America's Stake in the Pacific

Paul Seabury is professor of political science at the University of California, Berkeley. He has the Ph.D. from Columbia University. He is the author of a number of books on foreign policy, including *The United States in World Affairs, The Rise and Decline of the Cold War,* and *Power, Freedom, and Diplomacy,* which won a Bancroft Prize.

America's Stake in the Pacific

Paul Seabury

Foreword by Senator S. I. Hayakawa

Illinois Benedictine College
Theodore Lownik Library
Lisle, Illinois

Ethics and Public Policy Center
Washington, D.C.

THE ETHICS AND PUBLIC POLICY CENTER, established in 1976, conducts a program of research, writing, publications, and conferences to encourage debate on domestic and foreign policy issues among religious, educational, academic, business, political, and other leaders. A nonpartisan effort, the Center is supported by contributions from foundations, corporations, and individuals. The authors alone are responsible for the views expressed in Center publications.

Library of Congress Cataloging in Publication Data
Seabury, Paul.
  America's stake in the Pacific.
  Includes index.
  1. United States—Foreign economic relations—Pacific area.   2. Pacific area—Foreign economic relations—United States.   3. United States—Foreign relations—Pacific area.   4. Pacific area—Foreign relations—United States.   I. Title.
HF1456.5.P3S4   327.730182'3   81-2137
ISBN 0-89633-045-1   AACR2

$4.00

© 1981 by the Ethics and Public Policy Center. All rights reserved.
Printed in the United States of America.

Contents

FOREWORD *by S. I. Hayakawa* vii
PREFACE ix
MAP OF EAST ASIA xi
1 JANUS-HEADED AMERICA 1
2 AMERICA AND THE PACIFIC ECONOMY 5
3 CONFRONTING COMMUNIST ASIA 13
4 THE ROLE OF CHINA 22
5 STRATEGIC PERIMETERS IN ASIA 29
6 JAPAN: ALLY AND RIVAL 37
7 SOUTH KOREA AND TAIWAN: PROSPERING BUT THREATENED 47
8 TOWARD A SECURITY COMMUNITY 61

APPENDIXES
A. The Shanghai Communiqué (1972) 67
B. Joint Communiqué on the Establishment of Diplomatic Relations (U.S.-P.R.C., 1979) 71
C. Taiwan Relations Act (1979) 72

INDEX OF NAMES 81

Foreword

ONE OF THE FIRST ACTS of the new Reagan administration in February 1981 was to entertain South Korean president Chun Doo Hwan on a state visit to Washington. The United States, asserted its new President, "will remain a reliable Pacific partner" and "maintain the strength of our forces in the Pacific area." President Reagan pledged to keep 39,000 U.S. troops in the Republic of Korea, whose security and independence are menaced by a militant and militarily powerful Communist North Korea. These assurances toward the Korean peninsula and toward the Western Pacific in general contrast sharply with the policy exemplified by President Carter four years before when he announced his intention to withdraw all American ground forces from South Korea.

The concern over growing Soviet power reflected in the new U.S. stance was also in evidence in Japan, America's chief Pacific ally and the world's second-largest economic power. On February 7, 1981, for example, the Japanese government proclaimed "Northern Territories Day," and downtown Tokyo echoed with chants demanding the return of four northern islands that were seized by Soviet forces after World War II. Japan's defense budget is slowly being increased.

The free countries of the Western Pacific that are allied with the United States—Japan, South Korea, the Philippines, and, in a different sense, Taiwan—are endangered by the Sino-Soviet rivalry and by the threat of Soviet expansion. The conflict between Moscow and Peking threatens to spill over into other countries, especially in Southeast Asia. The modernized and growing Soviet fleet now has access to ports in Cambodia and Vietnam and poses a real and present danger to the maritime lanes.

South Korea is in special jeopardy; the highly militarized North makes no secret of its intention to "reunify" the peninsula, by force if necessary. "Reunification" also threatens Taiwan, though the People's Republic of China is exercising patience.

The keeper of the peace in the Western Pacific during the past three decades has been the United States. But it no longer can, and no longer should, carry the major part of this burden. America's military resources are now stretched thin. As the author of this study points out, the time has come for the prosperous free states in the region to accept a much greater responsibility for their own defense.

Thoughtful Americans should become more fully informed about America's strategic, political, and economic stake in East Asia. This study by Professor Paul Seabury, who teaches political science at the University of California, Berkeley, will help them do that. He has sorted the complex economic and political forces of the region, discerned their meaning, and recommended constructive courses of action for the United States and its Asian allies to take. His call for the creation of a Pacific security community is thoughtful and persuasive. I heartily recommend this well-researched and penetrating analysis.

S. I. HAYAKAWA
United States Senator from California

February 1981

NOTE: *Senator Hayakawa is the chairman of the East Asian and Pacific Affairs Subcommittee of the Senate Foreign Relations Committee.*

Preface

NOT BEING AN ASIAN SCHOLAR I am not familiar with all the cultural and linguistic taboos in this field. Certain expressions I use in this book will betray my innocence, others my cultural biases. Some words allegedly encode deep-set prejudices. I learned years ago, for instance, that "Asiatic" was best not mentioned. Although Dwight Eisenhower used it from time to time, in a casual sort of way, this word had become hopelessly linked with some pejorative terms such as "hordes" and "yellow peril."

Another expression I've been warned against is "Far East." To use it supposedly signals a clear pro-European bias, since that is what many Europeans say. But it certainly betrays no American chauvinism; as we Californians know, the "Far East" logically should be called the "Far West," or else the "Near East," since it is much closer to us than many a Middle or Near Eastern country, such as Afghanistan.

"The Orient," too, seems to have disappeared, except in the names of Chinese restaurants. I accept its demise, though it did have a certain exotic charm. I supose the reason it too had to go was its association with "Orientals"—who were thought to be "wily" or "inscrutable."

On a few other linguistic matters, however, I refuse to yield. I have not used the new transliteration system by which Chinese words are now decoded into English. The Peking authorities have told us to use this as a part of "normalization." In principle I have nothing against it; what annoys me is the inordinate difficulty of changing to it, as compared with the small improvements it promises. So in this book you will meet old friends again: Peking and not Beijing, Mao Tse-tung, Chou En-lai.

Whenever the phrase "the West" appears in this book I intend it to include not only America and European countries but also

ix

Australia, New Zealand, and Japan, even though Japan certainly is not Western but only partly "Westernized." By "the West" (and I can think of no adequate cultural substitute for it) I mean those countries whose peoples and governments share the cultural values that most Americans cherish, as do most Europeans.

I have also rehabilitated a fine expression that years of linguistic brainwashing have almost removed from polite conversation about world affairs: "the Free World." Some say it is a relic of the Cold War. But the global issues that gave rise to the term "Cold War" two decades ago persisted under the so-called détente and post-détente period. The Free World, fortunately, is still alive, and doing fairly well. In particular, as this book seeks to demonstrate, it is still alive and fairly well in East Asia.

PAUL SEABURY

December 1980

Map outline by permission of United Press International.
Lettering by Daniel F. Bonner, Ethics and Public Policy Center.

CHAPTER ONE

Janus-Headed America

THE UNITED STATES FACES both east and west, toward Europe and toward East Asia. Its security interests since World War II have lain in both these regions far more than in the rest of the Americas.

Whether America's deep involvement in East Asian affairs was inevitable or the product of historical accident, its status as a Pacific power today is incontestable. The United States has a long Pacific coastline. Two of its states are in the Pacific; this extends its strategic defense perimeter at least as far as Japan. And it is increasingly involved in the economy of the Pacific region—the fastest growing in the world.

An important difference between America's eastward and westward orientations is that it has powerful organic connections on the European side. The United States began as a colony of European civilization. It has long had a unique culture and distinctive attributes that sharply distinguish it from its European source, of course, and its attributes have been somewhat affected by the "American experience in Asia"; but it is bound to Europe by cultural connections and identifications, personal and family ties, intellectual affinities, shared experiences of victory and defeat. Despite the deep involvement of America (and Americans) in Asia since Pearl Harbor, a similar organic and sentimental connection has not emerged. America looks *out* on the Pacific; it looks *back* on Europe.

Americans can develop a faulty view of the world by envisioning it on a flat map with the United States at the center. This splits

Eurasia into two parts, one an Atlantic away from us and the other a Pacific away. It obscures the contiguity of the vast single superpower that lies across the northern reaches of both. From Central Europe the Soviet empire stretches through twelve time zones to the Bering Strait. It looms over Western Europe; it borders China along a heavily armed frontier of some seven thousand miles (a figure that includes the China border of Mongolia, a Soviet satellite); it lies scarcely fifty miles from Japan. An immensely powerful totalitarian state—the most militarily powerful in the world—lies at the junction of East and West.

Since the outbreak of World War II, Washington has faced profoundly difficult choices in establishing priorities between its strategic tasks in the Atlantic and its strategic tasks in the Pacific. After Pearl Harbor the U.S. choice was "Europe First": victory in Europe took precedence over victory in the Pacific. For three wartime years military activities in the Pacific were largely holding operations while U.S. resources were principally directed to Europe. In the immediate post-war years also, after the defeat of Japan, U.S. reconstruction aid flowed chiefly to war-devastated Europe. At the time of the Chinese civil war in the late forties, the prevailing opinion in the United States was that European political and economic recovery—and resistance to Communist expansion—lay within the reach of American resources while assistance to Nationalist China in its struggle against the Communists did not.

The reputation of General George C. Marshall is thus dramatically different in Asia than in Europe. The Marshall who led Truman's Marshall Mission to China in 1946 was assigned the impossible task of finding some way to reconcile Chinese Communist and Chinese Nationalist claims to control the mainland; the result was failure and Communist victory. The Marshall after whom the Marshall Plan was later named was credited with strengthening Western Europe's will to resist Soviet Communist expansion. The Truman administration apparently thought that U.S. resources could not be stretched to do on the Asian mainland what was being done in Western Europe.

Similar tensions arose during the Korean War (1950-53). After the North Korean invasion, important figures in the Truman administration regarded that attack as a Soviet attempt to deflect American attention from what was regarded as the central theater: Europe. This view constrained Washington's conduct of that war, particularly after the Chinese Communist intervention. The Truman-MacArthur controversy in 1951 arose in large measure from well-grounded fears that a widened war in Asia might cripple Western defenses in Europe; U.S. acceptance of a stalemate truce in 1953 was brought on by this view as much as by American reluctance to face a major conflict with Communist China.

Since the Vietnam War, the double standard in America's East-West orientations has been clearer than ever. For while there has been a general bipartisan consensus over U.S. vital interests in the defense of Europe against Communist expansion, this consensus has been far weaker with respect to Asia.

During the Vietnam War, many prominent Americans whose devotion to European defense was unshakable opposed U.S. involvement in Indochina. Some of them, like the late Walter Lippmann, eloquently argued that for the United States to become mired in Southeast Asia would weaken its resolve to defend the North Atlantic region. Such opponents of the war were by no means isolationist. Their opposition was rooted in a simple value judgment: Europe was more important to America than Asia. A significant bit of this bias persists, though the configurations of world politics have greatly changed.

Victory in Europe, Failure in Asia

America's collective memories of Europe contrast strikingly with its memories of Asia. In Europe, the success stories: successful containment of Soviet expansion, the successful Marshall Plan and the miraculous recovery of the European democracies, the success of bringing a new democratic West Germany into a free Europe, the triumphal Berlin airlift, NATO. And all these successes were achieved without the firing of a shot. Europe has enjoyed more than thirty years of peace; the line dividing totalitarian Europe from free Europe remains exactly where it was in 1948. While the shadow of Soviet military power hangs over all of

Europe more ominously today than in the past, Americans nevertheless can pride themselves on their unswerving commitment to the defense of Europe since World War II.

How different the memories of Asia! There the single unambiguous success story has been the nurturing of Japanese democratic elements into a sturdy society linked to the West. Other memories are far from pleasant. Asia, for Americans, has been the theater of two wars during the past three decades. One of them ended in a stalemate, the other in humiliating defeat. And now the mainland of East Asia, aside from South Korea, is dominated by two totalitarian powers.

Strategic success in Europe, strategic failure in Asia: this is deeply etched in the collective American memory. But how accurate is it?

In two senses the memory of the Pacific region is wrong. First, in strategic terms East Asia today is a region of multipolarity. No one Asian power dominates it, and this is how, from an American standpoint, things should remain. As long as a stable multipolarity is maintained, American interests will be well served.

Secondly, the non-Communist Western Pacific region is now a zone of peace that an American presence helps to sustain. This zone is one of remarkable economic growth and vitality. Intraregional economic ties, ties with Australia and New Zealand, and ties to the advanced industrial states of the West have woven these countries into patterns of cooperation that never before existed. Taken as a whole, the Pacific basin is becoming an economic zone of greater importance to the U.S. economy than Europe—a development of extraordinary historical importance. And the fortunes of this area depend in large measure on what political and strategic policies the United States pursues.

CHAPTER TWO

America and the Pacific Economy

NEO-MARXIST POLITICAL ECONOMISTS preach much about the persistent scourge of neo-colonialism in the world. To them, the salient characteristic of our world is its north-south division, which geographically segregates the rich from the poor. They see this pattern as simply a continuation of the historical domination by advanced Western societies of non-Western ones: a "center" dominates a periphery and dictates what it should produce, at low cost, to satisfy the center's wishes. And so the poor struggle to try to satisfy the luxurious tastes of the rich. The poor are hewers of wood and drawers of water, slaves to Western masters. This world-view feeds upon the latent emotions of Third World envy and a First World sense of guilt. Radical Marxists promote it in order to demand a new, "more equitable" system for distributing the world's goods. They call for global income redistribution through the taxation of peoples in the developed world.

This world-view fosters a distorted picture in which exploited confront exploiters, non-whites confront whites, the colonial non-West confronts the imperial West, and the burden is upon the West to make restitution for its past sins.* It obscures—or diverts attention from—certain profound changes in the world economy

---

*For a good summary of this problem see P. T. Bauer, *Western Guilt and Third World Poverty* (Ethics and Public Policy Center, 1977); for a fuller analysis, see Bauer's *Dissent on Development* (Harvard University Press, 1976) and Robert Tucker's *The Inequality of Nations* (Basic Books, 1977).

that cannot be fitted into its frame. Marxism cannot, of course, account for the great power of the OPEC nations, particularly those of the Arab-Persian Gulf. It rarely mentions the patterns of east-west economic power. And it rarely fits Communist-bloc states into the north-south configuration, for this would upset the neat division of northern capitalists and southern slaves.

More important, a Marxist world-view cannot account for the emergence of a new category of state, the "Newly Industrializing Country," or NIC. These dynamic nations—ten in all—in no way correspond to the stereotyped north-south pattern; they are widely dispersed throughout the globe. The dynamic ten are Brazil, Greece, Hong Kong, Mexico, Portugal, Singapore, South Korea, Spain, Taiwan, and Yugoslavia. If the world economy continues to prosper, the Philippines, Sri Lanka, and Malaysia may soon join the ranks. Some of these newcomers to modernity have moved from extreme poverty to wealth within three decades. Singapore, for example, was a poverty-stricken mudflat town in 1945; today its per capita income exceeds that of New Zealand. The NICs stand in contrast to stagnating or retrogressing state economies elsewhere, such as those of sub-Saharan Africa.

The neo-Marxist view has yet another flaw: it ignores the fundamental historical fact that trade and investment flow largely among advanced industrial countries, rather than between poor and rich ones. Other than buying certain raw materials grown or mined in tropical areas, the Western mixed-economy states have traded mainly with one another. Historically, global trade has been concentrated in the European–North Atlantic region. European decolonization in many parts of the world has been followed by chronic political instability, nationalization, civil and regional war, and mass expulsion, flight, or murder of "foreign" skilled workers, merchants, and entrepreneurs. All these factors contribute to economic retrogression or collapse. The recent economic history of such African states as Angola, Mozambique, Tanzania, and Uganda confirms this.

A development of great historical significance obscured by this Marxist north-south mythology is the emergence in the Pacific basin of a vast zone of industrial and commercial activity, rivaling the North Atlantic region as the center of the world economy. In this region economic relationships trace no well-worn historic routes; they criss-cross in random ways. The Pacific-basin economy has developed so quickly that the region has little regional consciousness. Its history remains to be written.

America: Hewer of Wood for Japan

Americans have recently become acquainted with one aspect of this new phenomenon: the Japanese economic miracle and its relation to the U.S. economy. Marxist students of neo-colonialism might study this U.S.-Japanese economic relationship, since it mocks their simple scheme of things. Capitalist America (the great world exploiter) ships primary products—grain, soybeans, rice, timber, and other raw materials—to Japan and in return gets Japan's cameras, stereos, TV sets, cars, and low-priced computers. In the first nine months of 1979, two new Japanese cars were sold in California for every three American ones. It costs less to ship cars from Japanese ports to San Francisco across 4,500 miles of the vast Pacific than to ship Detroit's models to the same address. To Japan, America is now a hewer of wood and a drawer of water!*

The United States has a new relationship to this region of the world economy. In 1979, for example, U.S. trade within the Pacific region for the first time in history exceeded in value its trade with Western Europe. This trend may be expected to continue.

Four of the "Newly Industrializing Countries" lie within the Pacific region: Taiwan, South Korea, Singapore, and Hong Kong. Taken together, their total exports of manufactured goods exceed by one-third the total export of manufactured goods of all the other NICs—Brazil, Spain, Portugal, Greece, Mexico, and Yugoslavia. They now enjoy growth rates far in excess of those of the more advanced industrial nations. All are essentially capitalist, free-market societies. Before World War II they were exceedingly poor; today some are on the threshold of affluence. All are close

---

*In 1979, for instance, foodstuffs and raw materials made up nearly three-fourths of the value of all U.S. exports to Japan. The chief U.S. exports to Japan in that year were grains and soybeans, wood and pulp, coal and coke, chemicals, aircraft and parts, and machinery. (See *Quarterly Economic Review of the U.S.A.,* 2nd Quarter 1980 [London: The Economist Intelligence Unit, 1980], Appendix.)

trading partners with the United States and provide profitable American investment opportunities.

This Pacific economy stretches from New Zealand and Australia to the East Asian region—including, on the way, the Philippines, Hong Kong, Taiwan, Japan, and South Korea—and to the western shore of North America. The United States is an intimate part of it. The Pacific economy does not include a single Communist state. Mainland China's trade with these other countries is minimal, as is its trade with the United States. Despite the renaissance of old romantic dreams about the China trade, there is small prospect that mainland China will become a major trading partner of the United States, and even less prospect that it will become a significant place for U.S. direct investment. American capital investment in Taiwan is now slightly above $4 billion, a figure that towers over the amount of American investment on the mainland. In a single year, 1978 to 1979, trade between the United States and Taiwan jumped from $7.3 billion to $10 billion.

Like the other Communist mainland states, China remains an economic basket case. Whatever its prospects for political stability may be, years of Maoist rule have taken their toll of the economy; the "Cultural Revolution" stripped it of an entire young generation of potentially creative leadership. To the south of China, the economies of Cambodia, Laos, and Vietnam lie in ruins. These Southeast Asian countries are plagued with military machines that overburden their economies. Vietnam's collectivization programs, its expulsion of ethnic Chinese, the flight of hundreds of thousands of Vietnamese, and the incarceration of hundreds of thousands more have made that country into a Soviet client state scarcely more attractive than its Cambodian enemy to the west. To the north, the North Korean Communist state, an armed camp, is isolated both from the Pacific region and from the larger world. Its economic performance pales in comparison to that of South Korea. The Pacific community of neighbors and trading partners thus lies wholly outside the Asian totalitarian camp.

Japan, of course, towers over the rest of the Asian Pacific nations. It is the principal trading partner of Thailand, Indonesia, Malaysia, and China, and it is the largest supplier to Singapore, the

Philippines, South Korea, Taiwan, and Hong Kong. Australian trade, once chiefly with Europe, has veered toward Japan, now its chief purchaser.

Productivity: The Westward Tilt

The dynamic Pacific basin poses new challenges, opportunities, and risks that as yet only a few perceptive economists have fully considered. Using straight-line projections, we could estimate that by the turn of the century the combined industrial power of Japan, Taiwan, South Korea, Hong Kong, Singapore, and Malaysia will far exceed that of the United States or Western Europe. Very possibly, the per capita income of these nations by then will exceed that of the United States, though this projection could be vitiated by political or economic events. By then, the center of the world's wealth (defined as productivity) will have moved decisively from its historical location to another one. (Interestingly, the westward tilt of the world economy toward the Pacific is mirrored within the American economy. The U.S. Southwest-West now enjoys growth rates comparable to that of the Japanese; the Northeast now resembles England. As energy costs continue to rise, this American tilt is likely to accelerate.)

This new international economic zone bears no resemblance at all to the mirage-like New International Economic Order so touted by United Nations bureaucrats, guilt-ridden liberals, and Barbara Ward humanists. For one thing, it is hardly an "order" at all. It has no organizational framework, no historic or cultural cohesion or ideology. The common denominator in the region, besides the absence of Communist control, is the marked shift toward liberal, market-spurred economic systems.

Yet this prosperous zone of economic strength owes its existence to something more fundamental than the initiative of entrepreneurs. Since 1945 the Pacific region has for the most part been a zone of peace. East Asian wars have been fought on the mainland; only during the first months of the Korean War was Pacific tranquillity seriously threatened.

The conditions both of mainland wars—Korea and Vietnam in

particular—and of insular stability made possible the development of the most unlikely country of the post-war period: Japan, whose own new state polity was based on the premise that, under American protection, it should not have the means of independently defending itself from attack. This curious condition could be understood only on the basis of a Pax Americana in the region. In the past three decades, Japan has emerged as the region's foremost economic power and the world's second-largest trading nation. The flourishing economies of Taiwan, Singapore, South Korea, and Malaysia have profited from the same U.S.-guaranteed stability, as have Australia and New Zealand to the south. (The Vietnam War, considered in its side-effects, amounted to a vast subsidy not only for Japan but for Taiwan and South Korea as well.)

In this larger context, the American defeat in Indochina was a defeat in battle, not a regional defeat. The *general* condition of order in the Western Pacific remains; it is only that the boundaries have receded. Had the United States been victorious in Vietnam, that country too might now be on the verge of affluence, instead of being an economic graveyard. As long as the strategic conditions of Pacific security remain, the region will continue to be an area within which investment capital—a shrewd judge of conditions—will operate according to the laws of a liberal, market-organized economic system.

The Growing Economic Challenge

This emerging Pacific basin creates for the American economy some serious problems of adjustment that we will ignore at our own risk. In the early post-war years, the Pacific regional economy was shaped and directed not so much by U.S. "orders" as by the sheer weight of American economic power. The economic changes wrought in occupied Japan, in South Korea, and in Taiwan during the height of U.S. influence there decisively affected the course of economic development, always deflecting government policy away from a heavy emphasis on state planning and nationalization. Capital investment gave special emphasis to export trade, and to manufacturing in highly competitive international markets.

Consequently, exports to the United States and other Western developed countries account for an ever-increasing proportion of the total exports of East Asian countries. And, contrary to the stereotypes of Marxist economists, these exports are by no means predominantly cheap raw materials. They are manufactured goods that compete directly with products manufactured in the United States. Americans have long been aware of Japan's manufacturing prowess. Now the Newly Industrializing Countries too are exporting manufactured goods. Their most successful products are textiles, clothing, electronic gadgets, transportation equipment, shoes, fishery products, and metals. Taiwan also has a flourishing shipbuilding industry that competes in markets for pleasure craft and other vessels. Both South Korea and Taiwan are seeking to move into high technology. Taiwan's research and development in electric automobiles is a portent of major industrial competition. South Korean automobiles now compete effectively in European markets; South Korean technicians play an important role in development projects in the Persian Gulf area.

The Newly Industrializing Countries are firmly committed to a truly international market economy. There is every reason to suppose that in the foreseeable future the NICs will be able to compete effectively in nearly every intermediate technology field.

The high performance and economic expectations of these states are, to a very large extent, contingent on their trade with the United States. That trade is increasing. Between 1970 and 1978, for example, U.S. trade with Japan, Taiwan, Hong Kong, Singapore, Malaysia, and South Korea increased at a rate of 17 per cent a year. The competitiveness of NIC products sparked clamors for protectionism even in industries where U.S. producers once had no rivals.

Initially, these developments took shape within an international economic environment where American dominance was virtually unchallenged. Today, while the United States remains the primary guarantor of peace in the Pacific, its economic leadership has steadily dwindled. Inflation, the decline in American productivity, and the declining dollar all attest to this. The new Pacific-region economy, devoid of regional institutions such as the Organization for Economic Cooperation and Development and the European Common Market, remains an amorphous zone of rivalry and cooperation; each component is deeply committed to a free international market economy, but each alone has little influence in seeing to it that this economy continues to flourish. NIC vitality still depends upon confidence in a continuing American military presence in East Asia. The faltering or collapse of this new economic region could have dire effects on the stability of the Free World.

CHAPTER THREE

Confronting Communist Asia

DURING RICHARD NIXON'S STATE VISIT to Peking in 1972, millions of Americans watching the "Today" show saw their President and First Lady, with Chiang Ching and the revered Chou En-lai, observing a performance in a Chinese Communist opera house. Dancing on the screen were lithe Chinese ballerinas in natty Red Army uniforms, rifles grasped like dowsing-rods as they solemnly searched out the last kulaks and remnant cliquers—a fastidious reenactment of the Revolution's grim mass murders. As the camera turned upon the audience, the American President was observed, his face wreathed in a polite diplomatic smile, applauding. (In his memoirs, Nixon recalls being "impressed by its dazzling technical and theatrical virtuosity.") Normalization had begun! (The text of the Shanghai Communiqué, issued at the close of Nixon's visit, appears as Appendix A of this study.)

As Americans look westward across the Pacific, what was once seen as a zone of hostile confrontation with a "monolithic" Communist world is now far more complex. The complexity started in the late 1950s, when the first signs of Sino-Soviet rivalry appeared. The Sino-Soviet split widened into a vast gulf of animosity and mistrust. Today that rivalry is a fundamental fact of world politics; above all it affects the strategic balance between East and West, between the Soviet Union and the United States. A healing of that breach could pose a grave threat to America's security and that of its allies. But Sino-Soviet war could also endanger world peace.

The complexity was compounded by the rapprochement between mainland China, East Asia's totalitarian colossus, and the West. Scarcely a decade ago the authorities of the People's Republic of China heaped scorn and abuse on the United States; now they welcome any assistance America can provide to help raise them from the ruins of thirty years of ruthless social experimentation and from their military weakness. Their emissaries in the West call for mobilization to resist Soviet "hegemony"; they are in the forefront of demands for a stronger NATO and greater West European solidarity vis-à-vis the Russians. They welcome Western science, technology, capital, and arms; Western scientists, engineers, businessmen, and defense experts obligingly respond with visits and contracts.

For its part, official America—for more than a decade well aware of many possibilities of Sino-Soviet conflict—has moved from a policy of cautious "equidistance" from the two Communist giants to one of unconcealed if limited favoritism. Meanwhile enthusiastic planeloads of American tourists debark in Chinese airports to fan out in carefully planned visits to villages and collective farms, archaeological sites, the Forbidden City, and, of course, the Great Wall.

Although Chinese officials' current candor about the economic shortcomings of their system contrasts sharply with propaganda of the not too distant past, many Americans on well-supervised visits would still have much the same general impressions as those related by Senator Mike Mansfield six years ago. In a report to the Senate that was an impressive example of selective perception, Mansfield said:

> The cities are clean, orderly, and safe; the shops well stocked with food, clothing, and other items; policemen are evident only for controlling traffic. . . . A casual sense of freedom pervades personal relationships with an air of easy egalitarianism. . . . The communes are . . . a new concept in social organization which acts to broaden and extend the virtues of interdependence of the old Chinese family system into a community of cooperation and group-action by many families. . . . In short, China has become a viable modern society which is rooted in the past, meets the needs of the present, and offers a soundly based hope for the future [quoted in Oscar Gass, "The China Policy," *The Washington Review,* April 1978, p. 34].

In their haste to "normalize" relations with the People's Republic of China, U.S. officials have paid a high price in concessions to Peking, as though America were a supplicant seeking recognition.

Herman Kahn has pointed to an interesting parallel between the Sino-Soviet tension in the Communist world and that great rift in Christendom known as the Reformation. In both cases the great conflict was a source of new life to the shared ideology. Even as Europe became the scene of violent discord and war over the faith, the faith flourished. Christendom spread as Catholic and Protestant missions, while at war with each other, recaptured their evangelistic zeal.

While Stalin lived and the Comintern was unchallenged by rival ideological claimants, Communist ideology was moribund. But Sino-Soviet rivalry inspired both parties, Moscow and Peking, to redouble their efforts to claim legitimacy in the world Communist movement. Their rivalry caused them to compete for the loyalty of revolutionary movements elsewhere, particularly in the Third World. This was vividly seen in the aid that both lavished on the Vietnamese Communists in the long Indochina war; at no point, for instance, did Peking seek to halt the flow of Soviet arms through mainland China to Hanoi. The American defeat in Vietnam was in large measure due to the tacit cooperation of the rival Communist giants.

Americans need to bear in mind three aspects of the strategic situation in East Asia that are rarely talked about. First, Communist Asia, considered as a whole, is today a gigantic armed camp. Second, these Communist states are all governed by totalitarian regimes whose disregard for human rights, while varying somewhat from country to country, stands in sharp contrast to conditions in non-Communist countries of the region.* Third,

---

*Americans continually fret about authoritarian practices in Taiwan or South Korea, which can easily be seen and protested. But rarely, if at all, does one hear protests of human-rights infringements in mainland China or North Korea, and for good reason: so tight is censorship there that absolutely no information is available on this subject. Amnesty International several years ago reported that, though it had "carefully monitored all available information from North Korea," it had come across "no detailed information whatsoever regarding arrests, trials, and imprisonment in that country."

significant threats to the peace in the area now emanate exclusively from these countries. The foreign policies of Japan, South Korea, Taiwan, the Philippines, and the non-Communist states of Southeast Asia raise no war alarms. The specters of general or regional war arise from the policies of the Soviet Union, mainland China, North Korea, and Vietnam. (Until 1979 Cambodia was on this list.)

Distracted by the Soviet arms buildup, Americans pay scant attention to the fact that this is a pattern common to all Communist states. The army of tiny, impoverished Vietnam, for instance, in 1979—five years after the end of the Vietnam War—numbered around one million, two-thirds the total number of U.S. ground forces at home and abroad. Now poised on the border of Thailand, Vietnamese forces exceed in number the combined army strength of Australia, New Zealand, Japan, the Philippines, Singapore, Thailand, Indonesia, and Taiwan. The mainland Chinese army of 3.6 million exceeds the Japanese self-defense forces by a ratio of twenty-five to one. The total ground forces of the United States, its East Asian friends, and significant neutrals in Southeast Asia (such as Indonesia) amount to approximately one-fifth of the total ground forces of the Communist states in Asia, including the Soviet Union.*

These staggering contrasts are not related to suggest Free World impotence, for mobility, technological capability, fire power, and skill as well as manpower are crucial. Nor is the comparison intended to suggest contemporary friend-foe juxtapositions. The comparison is made to underscore the high degree of militarization of Communist states compared to non-Communist states. All Asian Communist states are armed camps.

The Communist states have a common characteristic that dramatically distinguishes them from Free World countries and from all authoritarian states in the developed world: the ability to hide

---

*Data derived from the International Institute of Strategic Studies, *The Military Balance 1979/80*, republished in *Air Force*, December 1979. In East Asia, only Taiwan and South Korea maintain armed forces significantly large in proportion to their total population. Both, of course, have highly militarized neighbors that have made no secret of an intent to conquer them.

things from their own people. No domestic opposition is tolerated; no accurate information is publicly divulged about their military budgets, which consequently are subject to no form of public debate. Whatever information the Russian people have about the Soviet defense budget must be gained from Western sources. This is equally true of all Asian Communist states.

Free World countries, by contrast, have—or have the possibility of—publicly accountable governments; annual budgetary debates usually involve the guns-versus-butter controversy. Such debates do not occur in the Communist world, except in well-shrouded Politburo proceedings. Thus the tiny state of Vietnam, with an impoverished people, can maintain a military ground force two-thirds as large as that of the United States. In the United States the mere mention of compulsory military service—or even compulsory registration—evokes storms of disapproval.

The Free World: Militarily Inferior

This contrast between the Communist world and ours seems to be an enduring feature of world politics. Since the early 1950s, very few Westerners have entertained the slightest hope that these Communist regimes would be overthrown; none has been. The most Westerners have hoped for is that they might modify their character, and this has in fact happened in several Communist regimes in Eastern Europe, though not in Communist Asia. But whatever changes may have occurred in the repressive nature of Communist regimes, a constant feature is the enormous and increasing growth in their military power. The Free World—enjoying its affluence and its gentle permissiveness—is now militarily inferior to the Communist world. If the Soviet Union and the People's Republic of China should ever again become allies, the military inferiority of the Free World would be staggering.

For the time being, the military power of the East Asian Communist states is for the most part turned inward upon the peoples they control. The immense butcheries in Cambodia perpetrated by Pol Pot and the ensuing reprisals; the Communists' "consolidation" of their totalitarian rule in Vietnam; the brutal relocation of

Vietnamese peasants, bourgeois, intellectuals, and ethnic minorities; the unspeakable miseries of the boat people, who chose the perils of the sea to the life that awaited them on land; the Communist Vietnamese invasion of Communist Cambodia; the vicious punishment meted out by Vietnamese authorities to ethnic Chinese minorities—all these tragedies have taken place since the U.S. retreat and defeat in 1975 and under the shadow of the Sino-Soviet rivalry.

To some extent they are an aspect of this rivalry. Vietnam today is a Soviet satellite on the southern flank of China; its port facilities, notably Cam Ranh Bay, are now at the disposal of a rapidly growing Soviet Pacific naval force. Now that a pro-Soviet regime has been installed by Hanoi in Phnom Penh, Cambodian ports as well are open to the Soviet navy. Soviet nuclear submarines, probably operating from these ports, are poised in the nearby Malacca Strait, the vital maritime link between East Asia and the Persian Gulf.

To this catalogue of internecine warfare, administrative murder, and imprisonment must be added the possibility that Communist aggression will spill over into free Asia. As of late 1980, Communist Vietnamese units were invading Thailand in hot pursuit of Khmer Rouge units that were using it as a sanctuary. Far to the north, meanwhile, North Korean forces continued their experimental probes into the South, maintaining their determination to unify Korea under Communist control. No sharp distinction can be drawn between the Communist-inspired violence that points inward within Communist Asia and that which points outward toward vulnerable targets.

There are profound contrasts within this Communist world. In recent years the horrors of Cambodia certainly have had no parallel; Freedom House reported in 1978 that Cambodia was "perhaps the world's most complete tyranny." After seizing power in 1975, the Khmer Rouge killed millions of the Cambodian people. By comparison, Vietnam, after Hanoi's victory in 1975, would seem almost civilized. Hundreds of thousands have been sent off to concentration camps, hundreds of thousands of city-dwellers have been relocated to "new economic areas" to fend for themselves on the land, and hundreds of thousands have fled, by boat or otherwise. But at least the regime has not been guilty of genocide against its own people.

Brutalities in Post-Mao China

In East Asia Communism has brought about the same kinds of brutalities it earlier brought to Russia, including forced peasant collectivization, mass deportation of nationalities, concentration camps, the extermination of "reactionary" classes, rigid thought controls, meticulous police surveillance, the destruction of churches and monasteries, and other attempts to wipe out religion, whether Christian, Buddhist, or Confucian. Even at the present in post-Mao China, no foreigners—and possibly few Chinese themselves—have any idea how many political prisoners there are; according to reports from Chinese prisoners who escaped across the Soviet border, some of the jails make living conditions in Soviet labor camps appear comfortable by comparison. Marxism as a philosophical system may, as some philosophers argue, be dead; but Marxism-Leninism as a strategy of social engineering and brutal conquest is very much alive. In East Asia, Marxism-Leninism and the "struggle" to impose it have been savagely destructive of traditional and modern cultural elements. East Asian Soviet rule is less barbaric than the Chinese system, which to this day does not even have a penal code; the Soviets at least respect legality and due process as they define them.

Some observers argue that with Mao dead and the Cultural Revolution over, ruthlessness now may give way to more moderate modes of governance. This may be so; the Cultural Revolution may one day be recalled with the same horror with which Russians remember Stalin's terror. But it should not be forgotten that the savagery of the Cultural Revolution could not have continued indefinitely without totally destroying the fabric of the Chinese nation. The current leaders of mainland China—tough, idealistic, but pragmatic—are committed to modernization in ways that before would have been regarded as heretical; but they are equally committed to the maintenance of the power of the Party and in this sense behave exactly as did the post-Stalinist Soviet leaders, Khrushchev and Brezhnev.

To what extent have the new, more moderate Peking leaders abandoned their Marxist faith? To what extent, in particular, is their outreach to the West simply a tactic resembling the Maoists' collaboration with the Kuomintang in the 1930s against their primary enemy of the time, Japan? There is good reason to believe that the words of the late Mao Tse-tung, reissued in his *Selected Works* by the Peking leadership in 1977, retain their validity. Asserting the thesis that the goal of true Marxists was the destruction of capitalism, Mao said:

> In this matter we have no conscience! Marxism is rough, it has little conscience. It wants to extirpate imperialism, feudalism, capitalism, and small producers. In this matter it is good to have no conscience. We have some comrades who are too gentle, not severe; in other words, they are not very Marxist.

The current tendency among Peking officials, academics, and others to denounce the Cultural Revolution and the infamous Red Guards for the destruction they visited upon China in a way resembles the anti-Stalinist fervor that followed Nikita Khrushchev's de-Stalinization speech to the twentieth party congress in 1956. In both instances one chapter of the endless "revolution" is selected out as being deviant: Stalin is denounced, Lenin spared; the Gang of Four is denounced, Mao spared. What occurred *before* Stalin or *before* the Cultural Revolution can be forgotten.

But the savagery of what went before the Cultural Revolution is just as relevant to an assessment of Chinese Communism as the equally terrifying experiences of the Bolshevik Revolution in the early 1920s are to an assessment of Soviet Communism. Both in the Stalin terror and in the Cultural Revolution, what was most shattering to the Party was that the chief victims were Party members. Stalin liquidated them from the top; the Red Guards, from the bottom. Such stages as class liquidations, the extermination of religious faiths, and the execution of land owners had already taken place. After the Cultural Revolution, certain Party functionaries were rehabilitated. These, like Stalin's Party victims, were part of the machinery that earlier had purged the country of its reactionary elements. They are now in charge of the country.

Communist leaders—whether in Moscow, Peking, Pyongyang, or Hanoi—are all quite familiar with the contrast between their own closed systems and free societies. "The leaders are committed," as Richard Walker has pointed out,

> to maintaining their insulation against outside forces of any nature and at the same time exploiting the very pluralism and openness which characterize the systems on our side. *This is but one important reason why security in the Northwest Pacific has more than a strictly military dimension* [Korean-American-Japanese Conference on Northeast Asia (Report), July 5-6, 1977 (Seoul: Institute of East and West Studies, Yonsei University, 1977), p. 62].

An American "perimeter defense" in East Asia has three aspects: the containment of Communist expansion, the containment of Soviet expansion, and the containment of Chinese Communist expansion—a tall order indeed.

Illinois Benedictine College
Theodore Lownik Library
Lisle, Illinois

CHAPTER FOUR

The Role of China

HOW DOES THE PEOPLE'S REPUBLIC OF CHINA now relate to East Asian security? This question is one of the most complex ones facing the makers of U.S. foreign policy. In China, the United States and its Asian allies confront at once an ancient civilization; a totalitarian Marxist state that is far "less free" than America's chief adversary, the Soviet Union*; an impoverished land of one billion people; a power locked in rivalry with the Free World's most dangerous foe; a power that, denouncing "hegemonism," has hegemonic ambitions; and a regime whose own future is uncertain, to say the least. Recently hostile to the United States, China is now NATO's most ardent admirer and a staunch advocate of U.S. resistance to Soviet expansion everywhere in the world. Its diagnosis of the Soviet threat, while exaggerated and sometimes hysterical, contains elements of truth that Americans should acknowledge.

We must remember that for decades this giant Communist state has menaced its neighbors. It has fueled revolution and encouraged guerrilla warfare within India, Burma, Malaysia, Singapore, Thailand, Cambodia, Laos, Indonesia, Sri Lanka, and the Philip-

---

*According to a Freedom House report, in Communist China "there are no rights separate from the rights of the state and party. Rights to choose one's occupation, religion, or education are not acknowledged; even the right to be silent is often denied.... There may be millions of political prisoners, including those in labor reform camps.... Thirty million Chinese are systematically discriminated against because of 'bad class background' ..." (Raymond Gastil, ed., *Freedom in the World: Political Rights and Civil Liberties, 1978* [New York: G. K. Hall, 1978], p. 240).

pines. During the Indochina war, its support of Communist North Vietnam had the ironic and certainly unintended result of bringing Indochina under pro-Soviet Communist rule. Today, as Communist China searches for aid against the Soviet Union, its leaders refuse to disavow their world mission; specifically, they do not disavow support for revolutionary groups and movements in Southeast Asia.

Communist China, since Mao, has opted for what some have called the "Great Leap Westward." It now seeks military, technological, and economic aid from the advanced industrial democracies. China's new yet aging leaders admit that the country cannot conceivably modernize without extensive help from the "capitalist" world. One recalls a possible historical parallel, the Soviets' "opening to the West" in the 1920s. Then the Bolsheviks, also seeking to modernize, sought and got U.S. capital and technology. Private American firms such as the Ford Motor Company helped them build tractor factories, construct their steel industry, and electrify the country. Then, their jobs completed, the firms were expelled.

Communist Rivalry: A Boon and a Threat

The Sino-Soviet rivalry—which occasionally has moved to the brink of major fighting—poses a dilemma for America and its democratic allies. At its present level of intensity it certainly is a boon: it ties down forty-four Soviet divisions in Mongolia and Siberia, along the Chinese frontier. A reconciliation between Moscow and Peking could bring the combined might of the Communist world to bear upon their "capitalist" and "reactionary" enemies in Europe and Asia.

But the United States and its democratic allies have no interest in seeing that rivalry bloom into a full-scale war. Given Chinese inferiority in arms, such a war would be likely to change the global balance of power greatly in favor of the Russians. How would we respond? Our neutrality would cause us to concede Soviet dominance in East Asia; then the full force of Soviet power could focus on the West. Conversely, massive Western aid to China might lead down a slippery slope to full-scale world war. While the Soviets could not "win" such a war in the sense of conquering China, they could eliminate Chinese military power and potential for decades to come.

It is depressing to realize how much our fortunes are held hostage to this savage feud. How these two giant states will regulate their relations with each other is a matter that they and they alone will decide. It behooves us and our allies to do everything possible to free ourselves from dependence on this rivalry.

The Sino-American relationship came about because of the weaknesses of both countries. America, defeated in Southeast Asia and crippled by internal difficulties in the late 1960s and early 1970s, faced a China also gravely suffering from domestic troubles and faced by a very real threat of Soviet attack.

Since Nixon's China visit in 1972, America's relationship to China has moved through three stages: from hostility to a balanced "equidistance" from Moscow and Peking to the current position of undisguised favoritism toward Peking. No American secretary of defense has ever visited Moscow; Harold Brown's Peking trip in 1980 therefore seems truly symbolic of favoritism. Our interests and Peking's now are said to be "parallel." New circumstances could nudge the relationship toward even greater intimacy—or greater distance.

This new China relationship has had a disquieting effect on U.S. friends and allies in Asia. They view it in conjunction with America's declining presence in the Western Pacific region—its abandonment of the Republic of Vietnam in 1975, its "abandonment" of the Republic of China in 1978, and President Carter's decision, in 1977, to withdraw U.S. ground forces from the Republic of Korea (a decision subsequently and wisely suspended). Many Americans doubtless still regard the first of these abandonments as necessary, regardless of the immense loss of prestige it involved.*

---

*In his recent book, Richard Nixon quotes an Indonesian cabinet minister's remark, made just after the fall of Vietnam: "You Americans have lost your guts. You had the hell kicked out of you in Vietnam. You won't solve your energy problem. We'll make you pay and pay for oil. . . . Vietnam was your Waterloo" (Richard M. Nixon, *The Real War* [New York: Warner Books, 1980], p. 120).

The diplomatic abandonment of Taiwan and Carter's determination to dilute the U.S. security commitment to South Korea were unnecessary and unwise. The three, combined with America's new China policy, gave rise to severe apprehensions in East Asia: would a U.S.-China alliance against the Soviet Union replace the long-standing coalition of democratic and pro-Western Pacific-region nations, led by the United States?

Are American and Chinese interests really "parallel"? It is one thing to speak of ways in which states—friends or not—find some things to do side by side. It is another to see such states as moving on a common course.

Some American Sinologists, like Ross Terrill, consider the China connection good. The Chinese Communists are "our new friends." The People's Republic of China "promises to be a staunch partner in the containment of the Soviet Union."

A Sharply Limited 'Parallelism'

These views must be carefully scrutinized. To begin with, there is no parallelism, much less identity, between Peking's current world-view and ours. The official, as yet unrevised Peking concept of China's role in the world is hardly benign. Communist China presents itself as leader of oppressed nations of the world, rising up against the "imperialists" (a Communist way of saying "the United States"). The official Chinese view sees great-power competition in revolutionary terms: the United States and the Soviet Union strive for military dominance over each other; neither can attain it; a stable balance is therefore impossible; an uncontrollable arms race ensues; the Soviet Union is now the chief source of a new world war; this war *could* be postponed—perhaps indefinitely—by concerted measures to check Soviet expansion; but if these fail, war will come; when it comes, the world's peoples will rise in revolution; the Soviet Union and the United States will suffer "inevitable doom"; the war's outcome will be a victory for "socialism." China will survive such a war, even a nuclear one, because of its vast size, its numerous cities, and the defensive power of its militia. It will then inherit the true mantle of Marx and

Lenin and be recognized as the vanguard of the revolution.

This world view is an improvement over Mao's earlier doctrine, which viewed such an apocalypse as *inevitable*. But it is not much of an improvement. Even if we were greatly to discount it, there still are very many other concrete places where U.S. interests diverge, or should diverge, from those of the very "pragmatic" China we hear so much of. Let us make a survey.

There is indeed a slight parallelism between U.S. and Chinese interests, something that a decade ago no American could have believed possible. Neither China nor the United States wishes to see Southeast Asia dominated by Vietnam, and neither is pleased about the Soviets' naval access to bases both in Cam Ranh Bay, Vietnam, and in Kompong Som, Cambodia. This privilege enables the Soviets to interdict South Asian maritime routes. Neither China nor America would like to see Vietnamese power spread into Thailand; but now, in Cambodia, a Vietnamese rogue elephant stands poised on the Thai border.

This shared concern does not, however, result in parallel policies. China's way to check Vietnamese expansion has been to support Pol Pot's infamous Khmer Rouge; ours should be to press for the neutralization of Cambodia and to help Vietnam's neighbors stave off a further realization of the domino theory.* Here is where complications arise.

Vietnam's neighbors are also China's; for them, protracted Sino-American cooperation would magnify their long-standing fear of China. (The Indonesians, for example, have certainly not forgotten their close call in 1965, when the Chinese-supported Indonesian Communists almost succeeded in overthrowing Sukarno's government.) To make matters worse, the United States now has no really viable political presence in the area. For domestic reasons, including the influence of former anti-war activists in the Carter administration, Indochina has been a Washington bugaboo. Since 1976 U.S. activities in the region have been confined chiefly

---

*President Carter came close to accepting the Peking strategy in 1979, when the U.S. ambassador to the United Nations joined with China in voting to support Pol Pot's credentials—a cynical and unnecessary act of *Realpolitik*. The proper policy would have been abstention.

to giving humanitarian aid to survivors of Khmer Rouge massacres and to victims and refugees of Hanoi's purification programs. It is as though America had been reduced to the status of a giant international Red Cross, able to help nurse the wounded but unable and unwilling to play a role in bringing the massacres to an end. (There is a similarity between this apolitical humanitarianism in Southeast Asia and Washington's timid response to Castro's outrages in the Caribbean: we take in the victims.)

Peking: Still a Friend of Pyongyang

Little parallelism can be found in Washington's and Peking's policies toward Korea. Today, thirty years after the start of the Korean War, when American and Chinese troops fought and killed each other, one might hope that Sino-American "normalization" could be extended to encourage normalization in that bitterly divided country. At least, one might hope that Peking could normalize its own relations with the Republic of Korea. But Peking still reaffirms its support for North Korea, endorsing Pyongyang's claim to speak for Korea as a whole; and it continues to insist publicly that American troops withdraw from the peninsula, though there is some evidence that Peking sees the U.S. presence there as a barrier to Soviet expansion in the region.

Peking, of course, like the United States, has no interest in seeing another war erupt in Korea; yet such a war would doubtless start, as the previous one did, by aggression from the North. Peking's influence over Pyongyang is limited. If North Korean president Kim Il-sung were to exploit political turmoil in South Korea and attack, there is little likelihood that Peking could or would restrain him. More likely, fearful of direct Soviet support of North Korea in such a war, Peking would simply stay on the sidelines, giving rhetorical support. American diplomats in Peking in 1978, while eagerly bargaining away U.S. ties to the Republic of China, might then have insisted upon a quid pro quo in Peking's Korean policy; but they did not do so.

There can be no "parallelism" on the question of Taiwan, either. The United States insists that reunification take place peaceably, if at all; Peking insists that reunification occur in the 1980s. The two positions are not readily reconciled. Except for some catastrophic circumstance, no Chinese government in Taiwan would in the foreseeable future accept Peking's conditions for reunification, nor would any but a few of the Chinese on Taiwan who fled the mainland in the wake of the Communist conquest.

Two further cautionary notes. First, a China capable of matching Soviet strength in East Asia would also be an obvious danger to the free nations of Asia. This would be true even if Washington chose to establish more intimate ties with Peking. Second, never, in peacetime, has America allied itself with a major power that had expansionist aims. America's alliances since World War II have been exclusively with smaller powers that are on the defensive. A Sino-American alliance would be of a very different kind, one between autonomous near-equals—a relationship that the United States has had with no other power in its history.* This kind of alliance with an expansionist power, all too familiar to Europeans in the past, is dangerous.

Peking and Washington do agree on at least one thing: the Soviet threat to the international strategic balance. To the Free World, the Sino-Soviet rift is a boon. But to rely upon it, as on a crutch, is dangerous. Siding openly with China in that dispute would give unnecessary offense to the Soviets, at a time when we should be attending to Soviet adventures elsewhere. The United States and other free nations should be able to respond to the Soviet problems on their own. They have the resources, if not the will, to do so. How this might be done in the Pacific region will be the subject of the concluding chapter of this study.

---

*Some historians may quibble about this. In the 1790s, the United States and France were bound in an alliance concluded in 1777 during the American Revolution. But when revolutionary France in the 1790s rampaged through Europe and war with England broke out, President Washington for good reasons refused to honor the treaty, and instead proclaimed U.S. neutrality.

CHAPTER FIVE

Strategic Perimeters In Asia

WHERE SHOULD THE UNITED STATES draw its strategic perimeters—those forward lines inside of which we are determined to stand, and if necessary to fight? Policy choices like these are made not in a vacuum but in the crucible of world politics. They must take into account our interests and resources and those of our allies and adversaries.

The truce line across Korea, the so-called Demilitarized Zone, which is one strategic perimeter of U.S. forces in Asia, was the negotiated product of a devastating war. But the original 1945 border between North and South Korea at the thirty-eighth parallel was drawn by Soviet and U.S. military commands in one hasty session, to separate the occupation forces of the two sides pending the establishment of a unified Korean government. Americans at the time considered it a temporary administrative device. Today it remains a shield for the South against Communist aggression, though North Korea has violated this line in probing efforts by land and sea and continues to chisel long tunnels deep beneath the DMZ so its troops can invade by surprise.

Are peace and security well served when Great Powers shrink their strategic perimeters? In the abstract the question is unanswerable. In the case of U.S. strategic perimeters in Asia, recent history offers contradictory advice. On the one hand, when the Truman administration announced in early 1950 that the U.S. perimeter in Northeast Asia excluded Korea, American deterrence was severely diminished. The North Koreans accordingly launched their invasion of the South within months, assuming there would be no significant U.S. response, and Americans had their first taste of war on the Asian mainland. On the other hand, in the early 1960s the Kennedy administration drew its defense perimeter in Southeast Asia to include South Vietnam. Here a U.S. commitment was made but did not work, and America was involved in a second war on the Asian mainland. The latter of these two remembered experiences may account for the strange determination of Jimmy Carter to pull U.S. troops out of Korea.

In the making of commitments, security must take precedence over peace; otherwise one has neither peace nor security. But resources must be taken into account also. During hard times, states are sometimes driven by necessity to retrench—as did the United States after the Vietnam War, largely for domestic reasons. In such cases, commitments are reduced to correspond with reduced resources or a flagging will. In 1969 the Nixon administration concluded that it had a double task in Southeast Asia—to phase out the U.S. military presence and to negotiate a peace with Hanoi. It accomplished the first task and failed (again, for domestic reasons) at the second. The catastrophe that ensued is something most Americans would like to forget.

There was, however, one priceless by-product of the Vietnam War that was little noticed in the United States at the time. In 1964, when President Johnson got the Tonkin Gulf Resolution from Congress, there was a real likelihood that Indonesian president Sukarno, with Maoist support, would launch an aggressive war against Singapore and Malaysia. This reckless adventure was shelved when the United States massively intervened in Indochina. In September 1965, anti-Communist Indonesian military leaders, heartened by a strong nearby American presence, quelled a Communist *coup d'état* within the Sukarno government, destroying the pro-Maoist Communist party. This dramatic event radically altered the strategic picture in Southeast Asia outside Indochina. Today, Indonesia, Singapore, and Malaysia are at peace with one another, their foreign policies are pro-Western, and threats of Communist internal subversion are at a post–World War II low.

The main American strategic problem at the time of the Korean and Vietnam wars differs fundamentally from the main problem now. Then the specter was that of *simultaneous* Soviet and Chinese Communist aggression, in concert or in competition, against America and its allies. Today that is no longer a live threat.

The central U.S. strategic problem today is how to prevent Soviet domination of Europe, East Asia, and the Persian Gulf area. Were the Soviets to dominate any one of these regions, they could probably go on to dominate the others. Then the United States, thrown back across the oceans, would be a beleaguered North American bastion. In these grim circumstances the strategic problem would be simple: with no Asian or European allies, America's one remaining problem would be to prevent a direct attack on its homeland.

Another way in which today's strategic problem differs from the earlier one is that the new Soviet Union is far more powerful than the old, and its strategic reach extends far beyond the range it had in Stalin's time. It is now a global power: as Gromyko reportedly stated several years ago, no political issue in the world can be settled without the Soviets' active participation. And the Manichaean and messianic philosophy that inspires the Soviet leaders, as it does other Communist leaders, has in no significant way been modified.

When Strategic Perimeters Shrink

The retreat of a great power accompanied by a shrinking of its strategic perimeters, whether under duress or not, cries out for an explanation. The world—enemies, neutrals, and friends alike—watches, carefully scrutinizing the phenomenon: Is it a prudent consolidation? Does it foretell further retreat? Is it the beginning of general abandonment? Does it result in a widespread loss of credibility?

The Johnson administration's stubborn holding of Southeast Asia, until 1968, involving such a heavy expenditure of lives and fortunes (if not sacred honor), can be explained chiefly by a fear that failure in Vietnam would have repercussions elsewhere; and we can now see that this fear was justified. An America that had rescued South Vietnam, Laos, and Cambodia from the Communists and emerged with unimpaired morale would probably not have been so brusquely defied by Arab oil emirates. But by 1973, when this successful defiance began, the United States was sending unmistakable signals to the world at large that its days of "intervention" were over. Later President Carter was to say that we would not be motivated by an "inordinate fear of Communism."* We would desist from forceful intervention in other societies and would trade valuable assets with all, in a new and peaceable world. There would, however, be U.S. pressure to reform the internal practices of certain other states under the banner of Carter's "human rights" crusade.

As U.S. power was diminished in Southeast Asia in the early 1970s, two doctrines and one diplomatic coup helped prevent the retreat from becoming a rout across the Pacific. Each of these was a product of the Nixon White House. Both Nixon and Kissinger—as early as January 1969—were profoundly aware of the rapidly spreading domestic sentiment against U.S. involvement in Vietnam. They knew that this sentiment, reinforced by the alarming rise of cultural alienation and nihilism in America's upper classes, threatened to cripple America's new international position. In their view a new formula was required that could stop the U.S. retreat and restore some degree of domestic tranquillity.

In the past, statesmen have conjured up images of world order that would enable them to adjust to new circumstances gracefully. In 1826, George Canning, the British foreign secretary, faced with the twin facts of the U.S. Monroe Doctrine and the successful rebellions against Spanish rule in South America, proudly announced to Parliament: "I called the New World into existence to redress the balance of the Old."

The two doctrines that helped to keep the U.S. retreat from Southeast Asia from becoming a rout were embodied in President Nixon's Guam statement of 1971—subsequently called the Nixon

---

*See his Notre Dame speech in *Morality and Foreign Policy: A Symposium on President Carter's Stance,* Ethics and Public Policy Center, 1977.

Doctrine—and his declaration in 1972 of the five pillars of world order; the diplomatic coup that helped also was reconciliation with Communist China. The first of these three was policy; the second, like Canning's, constructive fiction; the third, a crutch. Each at the time had its justifications. And all three, to some degree, persisted as U.S. policy after Nixon's resignation.

The Nixon Doctrine: 'No More Vietnams'

The Nixon Doctrine and the ambiguous consequences that flowed from it can best be understood through Nixon's own later description of it in his memoirs:

> I stated that the United States is a Pacific power and should remain so. But I felt that once the Vietnam war was settled, we would need a new Asian policy to ensure that there were no more Vietnams in the future.... We would keep all our existing treaty commitments, but ... we would not make any more commitments unless they were required by our own vital interests.
>
> In the past our policy had been to furnish the arms, men, and materiel to help other nations to defend themselves.... But from now on ... we would furnish only the materiel and the military and economic assistance to those nations willing to accept the responsibility of supplying the manpower to defend themselves [*RN: The Memoirs of Richard Nixon* (New York: Grosset and Dunlap, 1978), pp. 394, 395].

Simply stated, the Nixon Doctrine entailed the gradual reduction of direct U.S. force deployment in East Asia, so staged as to be balanced by the development of compensatory strength in U.S. allies. But no sooner had the doctrine become known than some observers perceived it as an announcement of Washington's decision to withdraw completely. Nixon later recalled that the Senate majority leader shared this misunderstanding:

> The Nixon Doctrine ... was interpreted by some as signaling a new policy that would lead to total American withdrawal from Asia and from other parts of the world as well. In one of our regular breakfast meetings ... Senate Majority Leader Mike Mansfield articulated this misunderstanding. I emphasized ... that the Nixon Doctrine was not a formula for getting America

out of Asia, but one . . . for America's staying *in* and continuing to play a responsible role in helping the non-Communist nations . . . to defend their independence [*Memoirs,* p. 395].

Then Senator Mansfield, doctrine in hand, enlarged upon it, calling for Senate approval of his own version that entailed the withdrawal of U.S. troops from Europe as well. While that venture miscarried, the Mansfield corollary was to live on both in Senator George McGovern's campaign for president in 1972 and in certain subsequent policies of the Carter administration.

The 'Five Pillars' of World Order

Nixon's second contribution to readjustment can best be summarized in his Canning-like depiction of a new basis for international order—a constructive fiction composed more of his own aspirations than of reality. As he described this to a *Time* magazine reporter in 1972, the world order he saw emerging was to be sustained by five pillars: the United States, the Soviet Union, China, Japan, and Western Europe. As these powers jointly addressed common global problems, acting in restraint in their relations with one another, the world could advance. After this doctrine became widely known, a Chinese Communist official asked an American businessman some questions:

> Did this portrait truly reveal underlying official American thought? Did unofficial Americans generally believe these five poles to prevail? . . . But before anything else, does five *poles* mean the same thing, to you Americans, as five *great powers?* Is this different language due only to developments that have made your people shy away from the power that comes out of the barrel of a gun? [Oscar Gass, "The China Policy," *The Washington Review,* April 1978, p. 30].

The Chinese official's incredulity is understandable; the edifice sustained by such supports would be more like a sand castle than a Gothic cathedral.

If these were *powers,* they were of very different kinds. One of them, Western Europe, had no common government; another, Japan, had a constitution that virtually forbade any exercise of military power other than shore defense; a third, China, was a totalitarian backward giant with an antiquated army and vast domestic problems, and little capacity to project power save to adjacent regions. That left the United States and the Soviet Union. Could the President of the United States have taken his five-pillar formulation seriously?

Yet what a relief it was to get rid of the old, dangerous bipolar world, the Cold War world, by calling into being a nice pentagonal one. Many hands make light work. The tiring American Atlas would find its assignment more modest now that others were helping out. Like Canning, Nixon called into being a new world, to replace the dangers and burdens of the previous one. But the question put to Owen Glendower in Shakespeare's *Henry IV* comes to mind:

Glendower: I can call spirits from the vasty deep.
Hotspur: Why, so can I, or so can any man;
But will they come when you do call them?

In fairness, Nixon should be credited with some Asian accomplishments. He prevented America's retrenchment in Asia from turning into a rout. His reconciliation with Communist China was aimed at making an American presence in East Asia acceptable to what only recently had been America's most implacable ideological foe in the region. (It is instructive to recall the savage ideological controversy between Mao and Khrushchev in the early 1960s. The most heretical feature of Soviet revisionism, to Mao, was its abandonment of the doctrine of the inevitability of war and its assertion that in a major nuclear war both "socialism" and "capitalism" would suffer. Mao insisted that Communist China could both survive and win a nuclear war; capitalism could not.)

The rapprochement between the United States and Communist China was made possible by the difficulties each had—Peking, its grave crisis on the Soviet border; Washington, its domestic crisis over foreign policy and the winding down of the Vietnam War. It is clear that, at least from Washington's view at the time, the new relationship was not intended to be an alliance against Moscow. Nixon intended it as a policy of "equidistance," a part of his larger scheme of détente, and took pains to portray it as such. In the framework of détente, a relationship with Peking in Asia would be wholly compatible with a policy of relaxation with the Russians in Europe over arms control and other weighty matters. The Russians were so informed.

Furthermore, to put a good view on it, "normalization" with Peking would have the additional side-effect of "legitimating" what remained of the U.S. presence in Asia. Peking's previous ceaseless pressure to get Americans out entirely was halted for the time being, for the American presence in a time of great danger to China could be seen as a countervailing power in Asia. Peking's attitude became more positive as its relations with Moscow worsened and its military inferiority became more apparent. Soon it began calling for a stronger West and a stronger America, a stronger European Community and a stronger NATO.

This Sino-American rapprochement inspired contradictory reactions among America's Asian allies. Relations with Japan were strained by the surprise Nixon visit, of which our chief Asian ally had had no advance notice. The so-called Shanghai Communiqué, which defined our accommodation with Peking and papered over remaining differences, precluded one U.S. option in the China-Taiwan dispute, a two-China policy, and raised the specter of U.S. abandonment of the Republic of China. Further, the Sino-U.S. rapprochement raised the disturbing possibility—which Nixon's assurances to the contrary could not dispel—that it might slip into a de facto anti-Soviet alliance and thus serve as a substitute for a strong U.S. presence in Asia. Such an alliance would certainly mean that U.S. Asian policy to some extent would become hostage to the interests and ambitions of the world's largest totalitarian power.

CHAPTER SIX

Japan: Ally and Rival

To most Americans today, Japan is where the cars, TV sets, and stereo systems come from. As consumers, we approve; as producers, we view Japanese industry with alarm. One by one major American firms have fallen before the might of this efficient and resourceful economic giant. Many Japanese, deeply concerned by the rebirth of American protectionism, recall the 1930s, when U.S. tariffs and import quotas severely damaged Japan's export industries. Some also fear that economic hostility may tear apart the close political and military bonds between the two countries.

This is ironic, because America has been Japan's chief tutor in economics and technology. Strategically, Japan has been America's principal ward and ally in the Pacific for more than thirty years. Moreover, the United States and Japan today have closer common interests and world-views than at any time in recent history.

The extraordinary bonds of solidarity between the two are the biggest success of post–World War II American diplomacy in the Pacific region. This close relationship is essential both to Free World security and to future economic growth in the area. Its continued vitality depends upon a highly sensitive calibration of diplomacy by both countries.

Since the Korean armistice in 1953, the security and peace of the Western Pacific have been sustained through a balance of power in which the United States has played a key role as deterrent and peacekeeper. America's security pact with Japan is the core of a broader *de facto* system of security embracing South Korea, Taiwan, Okinawa, and the Philippines. From a strictly military point of view we might speak of the Korea-Japan-Taiwan zone of

East Asia as the "iron triangle" for regional security. While the U.S. presence eroded considerably in the 1970s, it has by no means disappeared, and some observers would regard it as more important now than ever before.

As Zbigniew Brzezinski pointed out in 1972, "for many years America has been both Japan's roof against rain and its window in the world." To put the matter differently, Japan's unique post-war role in the world has depended hugely upon its confidence in U.S. security guarantees. Without them, Japan today would be playing a very different role.

The U.S.-Japanese relationship is without parallel in the history of world politics. Never before has a defeated great power so totally and eagerly accepted client status under its conqueror. (In Japanese polls, Americans are still regarded as Japan's best friends.) Nor is there any other example of such a country's subsequently becoming a major economic power in its own right, though in no way aspiring to match its economic strength with political influence. Japan's almost unqualified acceptance of a role as a power rejecting power politics is striking

Also interesting is the ease with which Japanese citizens accepted the civic values imposed upon them by their conqueror. Japan today is a stable democracy whose constitution was written and handed down by its occupying authorities. One might have expected a nationalistic backlash against such an alien decree, but there are few signs of such sentiments except in Japan's radical left, the only segment of the population where anti-Americanism flourishes.

Japan's eager renunciation of power politics is often attributed to the combination of its total defeat in 1945 and the benign and constructive U.S. occupation. Japan became the sole victim, to date, of modern and nuclear war. For all other countries, nuclear war remains hypothetical; for Japan, the holocaust of Hiroshima and Nagasaki was all too real.

The invasion of Manchuria and the subsequent attack on Pearl Harbor were a part of Japan's only expansionist adventure, one that was brief, uncharacteristic, and catastrophic. Before the late nineteenth century, Japan—save for its incursions into Korea—

had no experience with imperial "greatness." And it had never experienced invasion and occupation by a foreign power. The one attempted invasion of Japan by foreigners—a Mongolian attack by sea—occurred more than 600 years ago and miscarried when a great storm devastated the Mongol fleet. (The Japanese term *kamikaze*, which Westerners associate exclusively with World War II Japanese suicide pilots, derives from that episode; the gales that did in the Mongols were "divine winds," *kamikazes*.) The history of all other major powers abounds with great tragedies and triumphs, defeats and victories, and courageous exploits in arms. Japan's history is singularly free of these momentous events.

Japan's imperial ventures were confined to two generations. There is therefore precious little justification for dubbing them "closet imperialists" who are awaiting a chance to resume old expansionist habits. In fact, the absence of imperial design creates a quandary for Japanese leaders genuinely concerned for the security of their country. Japan's long tranquillity as an island fortress was its good fortune—but not a good apprenticeship for its position and responsibility in the world today.

Renouncing War 'Forever'

Article IX of the U.S.-written Japanese constitution symbolizes the dilemma of Japan in world and regional politics. In it, Japan "forever" renounces war as a "sovereign right." While this clause has been interpreted to admit the right of self-defense, it remains a powerful inhibition to a larger security role.

The clause was included to advance the U.S. objective of total Japanese demilitarization. But its authors, General Douglas MacArthur and his deputies, were later to regret their success. They could not anticipate how eager post-war Japanese leaders would be—and for how long—to clutch this imposed constraint to their bosoms.

One wonders how Washington developed the strange idea of a permanently demilitarized Japan. History shows that the permanent neutralization of a great nation is possible only when there are trustees of its security and guarantors of its demilitarization. A disarmed, neutralized nation undefended by an outside power is an invitation to trouble. Washington may have failed to recognize that it would have to be both trustee and guarantor and thus the inheritor of Japan's security problems. For example, Korea historically was seen as a "dagger" pointing at the heart of Japan; henceforth Korea would point at the heart of American vital interests also. Japan's classical problems with nearby China and Russia would be America's also.

And so the United States, having tutored its former enemy to renounce military might, was soon pleading for Japan to renounce its renunciation. The Korean War was the occasion for this sudden reversal, though it would have happened anyway. But the abject, conquered nation now in effect served notice that it wished to remain abject. A Japanese foreign minister, Mamoru Shigemitsu, insisted that Japan would continue to be a passive state, acted upon by others but not acting upon others, determined in no way to influence or interfere in the affairs of other countries. (See Franz Michael and Gaston Sigur, *The Asian Alliance: Japan and United States Policy* [National Strategy Information Center, 1971], p. 1.) John Foster Dulles in the 1950s pleaded with the Japanese to put their boots back on, and U.S. diplomats have done so ever since, but in vain.

Protecting a Prosperous Giant

A source of acute embarrassment today is that the United States, whose strategic and economic resources are strained to the breaking point, goes on at considerable cost to protect a prosperous economic giant that threatens to overwhelm the American economy. In 1979, economic analysts began to suspect that Japan's GNP already exceeded that of the Soviet Union. If this is true, Japan now has the world's second-largest economy. But it devotes less than 1 per cent of its GNP to defense, and such armed forces as it does maintain are solely for self-defense. The United States devotes nearly 6 per cent of its GNP to defense and has obligations extending around the world. (Note, of course, that the U.S.-Japanese security treaty of 1960 obliges the United States to defend Japan; there is no reciprocity, aside from Japan's presumed cooperation with its defenders.)

In the jungle of world politics, Japan's strategy has been to remain friendly with all. A former Japanese foreign minister, borrowing a term from judo, expresses it as the doctrine of *happo-yabure*, defenseless on all sides. He explains that this means a "diplomatic policy of being friendly with everybody, or at least not making serious enemies anywhere."

A corollary is the policy of not building up military forces lest these be seen as a threat by some other country. Japan's self-defense forces are professional but small. They are designed to deal with threats below the level of direct assault on the home islands, and successive Japanese governments have set severe limits upon both the quantity and the quality of arms needed for these limited purposes. Zealously banned from the Japanese arsenal are all categories of arms that could be perceived—by Japanese or others—as offensive weapons. Likewise, the Japanese capacity to project power is severely constrained. "Several hundred miles" is the range currently mentioned by Japanese strategic authorities as the limit beyond which even Japan's naval might should not stretch.

Japan's defense policy depends upon three factors: détente among the other major world powers (or at least no serious confrontation); a continuation of Japan's "special relationship" with the United States (meaning, of course, a credible U.S. strategic presence in East Asia); and the persistence of a vibrant world market economy tolerant of Japan's astonishing productivity. That economy must guarantee Japan both access to world markets and the imports that are vital to its survival (over 80 per cent of its energy is imported; 60 per cent of its oil comes from the Persian Gulf).

If any one of these three conditions changed significantly, Japan would face a profound security dilemma and a major internal political crisis. Most Japanese political leaders today acknowledge these realities, though they have not done much to cope with them.

Why should this economic giant continue as a ward of American strategic protection when it contributes so little to security in the

Pacific area? We can understand the reasons for the "free ride," for Japan's lack of any significant strategic support in East Asia, but we must not allow our comprehension to be misconstrued as approval.

American strategic defenses in East Asia, the Persian Gulf, Europe, and elsewhere guard the vital lifelines that enable Japan to exist as a large, prosperous country. Without this protection, Japan could become an economic cripple or a political hostage. As the Iran crisis has shown, Japan already is menaced by grave strategic changes in an area far beyond its "several hundred mile" limit. A major U.S. diplomatic challenge is how to make the Japanese understand these realities before American popular resentment grows even larger, and without sparking a major domestic crisis in Japan. Any Japanese government would, of course, be loath to give up its thirty-year low-profile policy. Moreover, for Japan to become a burgeoning military power would send shock waves through East Asia. This would have unpredictable consequences *unless* it were perceived as part of a much larger scheme of regional collective security.

A second challenge facing American diplomacy is to reassure the Japanese (and other East Asians) that the decade of steady American withdrawal from Asia has come to an end. The Carter administration's callous "abandonment" of Taiwan and flirtation with troop withdrawals from South Korea raised specters in Japanese minds of wholesale American abandonment of the area. And even if U.S. intentions have now changed, the resources available for regional security are sorely stretched. Since the Persian Gulf has become a crisis area, Washington has drawn heavily from its Seventh Fleet to beef up its presence in the Middle East.

Few Japanese, no Americans, and none of America's allies wish to see a powerful, non-aligned Japan whose military force fully reflects its economic might. This prospect would be far more likely if Washington really withdrew from East Asia. Japan's predicament would then be clearly visible. It would have three choices: Finlandization (neutralization), which would mean coexisting by the sufferance of its Soviet neighbor; joining its destinies with its beleaguered Chinese Communist neighbors; or becoming an island bastion bristling with arms and inhabited by an insecure and probably deeply divided people. Given the global reach of Soviet naval power, neither of the latter two choices would provide for the security of vital maritime routes. (Both Taiwan and South Korea would face the same unpalatable choices if U.S. power were withdrawn.)

Needed: A New Security System

Clearly, a new defensive security system in East Asia is needed, one that is independent of mainland China and essentially collective in nature. In this, U.S. power, especially at sea, would be augmented by and interact with the assets of free states in the area. Under this collective security arrangement Japan could act in concert with other powers (including the United States) in extending its strategic perimeters, without being or being perceived as a threat. Linked with friendly independent states, Japan could become a co-guarantor of Pacific tranquillity. Peking would find this a painful pill to swallow, but it would not choke.

All this is easier said than done, of course. The Japanese have good reason to be wary of surprises from Washington. They remember the Nixon shocks of the early 1970s—America's sudden about-face toward China and Nixon's surprise new monetary policies of 1971, both initiated with no previous diplomatic consultation; they remember the sad scenario of American disengagement in East Asia; they are aware of the waning strength of the U.S. naval presence in the Pacific; they witnessed the many vacillations and inconsistencies of U.S. policy during the Carter administration. Japanese opinion polls show that only a small minority continues to believe that Washington would defend Japan as it is obligated to do under the bilateral security treaty.

But there is a ruthless logic in historical circumstances. In an important sense, Japan has no viable options other than to play a much more active global diplomatic role. Japanese rearmament is inevitable; what remains to be seen is what form it will take, how soon it will occur, and what circumstances will prompt it. Politically speaking, the only way in which Japan can play a larger, constructive role regionally is within a comprehensive security system.

Much can be done without dramatic pronouncements. Joint planning between U.S. and Japanese defense authorities is already occurring; Japanese warships already have ventured outside their territorial waters in joint fleet maneuvers near Hawaii; Japan already has shown signs of willingness to use its tremendous economic assets to bolster unstable economies in Southeast Asia and even as far afield as Egypt and Turkey; and the Japanese are developing increasingly intimate ties with Australia and New Zealand. The conditions for an "organic" Pacific security system are already present. What Japan needs most of all is the clear assurance that the U.S. retreat from East Asia has ceased—indeed, has been reversed.

'High Politics' vs. 'Low Politics'

Scholars sometimes distinguish between "high politics" and "low politics." High politics includes matters of state security, national interests, and questions of war and peace, while "low politics" refers to such seemingly mundane matters as commerce, investment, and cultural exchange. In the everyday world, the low and the high are invariably intertwined; sometimes, as now in the matter of oil imports and other energy considerations, the low is almost indistinguishable from the high goal of national survival. Yet the distinction remains useful.

For reasons of state, matters of low politics are often used for high purposes; for instance, a government may encourage trade and investment to further important political and strategic purposes. Sometimes, too, a government may put up with the commercial and investment policies of a valued friendly partner even when those policies are adverse to its own economic well-being; they may be tolerated as a price of friendship and support on more important matters.

Today U.S.-Japanese commercial friction intrudes heavily upon high politics. The proximate causes of this friction are obvious. The United States, since World War II the world's most prominent advocate of a liberal world trading community, now faces in Japan the world's most prominent beneficiary of this principle. Japan, by now perhaps the world's second most productive economy, is probably also the world's most competitive one. The discipline and skill of the Japanese work force are matched by the extraordinary ingenuity of its management and technologists. Sector after sector of the U.S. economy has fallen prey to the competition of Japanese products. In the strictly bilateral relationship of our two countries, America has virtually become the hewer of wood and drawer of water for Japan, and Japan supplies our market with goods that once were the very hallmarks of American supremacy in world markets. After years in coming, the crisis hit the U.S. automobile industry with a bang. Imports from Western Europe also added to the shock.

There is some truth in the repeated allegation that Japan's superior economy is the consequence of its "free ride" as a security client of the United States. For three decades the Japanese have drawn on their economy hardly at all for defense purposes. Yet it is by no means indisputable that Japan's comparative strength today would be less had it chosen a different course. The competitive decline of American industry can also be observed in relation to the economies of other countries, such as West Germany, whose defense burden is far heavier than Japan's.

The commercial friction between U.S. manufacturers and Japan owes much to glaring American shortcomings, not the least of which is the sharp decline in productivity and in commitment to the work ethic, the lagging entrepreneurial talents of American exporters, and the waning of research and development talents in U.S. industry. Certainly no American businessman can attribute much of America's lag in comparison with Japan to environmental constraints; Japanese industry has borne as great a burden, if not a greater one, from such regulations. (See Adam Myerson, "Japan: Environmentalism With Growth," *Wall Street Journal,* September 5, 1980.)

A former Japanese foreign minister observed that "some Japanese look to the American economy in a little of the same spirit that the [prudent] ant reproached the [imprudent] grasshopper in the fable of Aesop." Americans' bent toward lavish consumption rather than savings and investment, he pointed out, is a major cause of their country's declining economic strength (Saburo Okita, "Japan, China and the United States," *Foreign Affairs*, Summer 1979, pp. 1092-94).

There is, however, one very large and generally overlooked way in which Japan has benefited economically from its one-sided security relationship. Both as private consumers and as military purchasers, U.S. defense personnel in the Western Pacific have spent vast amounts of money on Japanese goods and services. This infusion of U.S. capital has helped to make Japan's economic growth the miracle it is today. Here, Japanese "low politics" clearly benefited.

Moreover, in the interest of "high politics," U.S. administrations from Eisenhower's onward have tolerated a glaring asymmetry in commercial practices. Japanese firms have been allowed much easier access to U.S. domestic markets than the Japanese have accorded to competitive American firms and goods.

The "law of the conservation of problems" holds that a solution to one problem gives rise to other problems. An object of U.S. diplomacy was to help nurture a free, democratic, and prosperous Japan—the very one that now presents itself as America's chief industrial competitor. Now, as we encourage Japan to play a new, positive role in regional security, we must anticipate an almost inevitable consequence of this role: it will generate important alliance problems for which Americans are not psychologically prepared. The replacement of the classic "low profile" Japanese foreign policy by an activist one will mean the end of America's hegemony in U.S.-Japanese security relations. The new arrangement, whether it works well or ill, must become a partnership of equals. The time will necessarily come when Washington will no longer be able to proclaim and embark on new courses of action in East Asia, assuming that its chief ally in the Pacific will obediently acquiesce.

CHAPTER SEVEN

South Korea and Taiwan: Prospering But Threatened

PRESIDENT EISENHOWER MADE A SERIOUS SLIP of the tongue when at a press conference in 1959 he casually described the Berlin situation as "abnormal." As soon as the words left his lips Soviet propagandists seized them and ran. Of course West Berlin was abnormal! Such a ridiculous enclave, so absurd a geographic deformation, so unnecessary a source of tension! West Berlin should be normalized by being absorbed into its surrounding socialist environment. Khrushchev turned the screws a bit tighter. In the 1962 Berlin crisis, Western supporters of West Berlin's freedom were accused of being unreasonable and unrealistic: hadn't Eisenhower himself said as much?

Political "abnormalities" can always be found in any part of the world, but the most dangerous of them have been the divided states: Germany, Korea, and China. Each in its own way is a product of World War II and the subsequent Cold War rivalry between the Communist world and ours. Germany and Korea were originally divided as zones of Western and Soviet military occupation and China, in 1949, as a consequence of its own civil war. In each case the separation was mistakenly thought to be temporary: unity would follow a peace treaty after which occupation forces would withdraw. In 1949 even the Truman administration thought it was only a matter of time before Chiang Kai-shek's battered legions on Taiwan would collapse and the Communists would occupy the island. Secretary of State Dean Acheson remarked in regard to recognition of Peking that Washington was simply "waiting for the dust to settle," the implication being that recognition was sure to happen. The Korean War and Chinese intervention put an end to that expectation.

Each of these divided nations—Germany, China, and Korea—straddles the frontier between a civil world and a despotic one. Their national fates are linked to the fortunes of two vast political realms, the Communist world and the Western world. Each part of the divided nations has taken on the color and character of the world—free or totalitarian—to which it belongs; the two parts are less like each other than like certain neighboring nations. West Germany, like its West European allies, is a constitutional democracy; the Republic of China on Taiwan and the Republic of Korea, though partly authoritarian, enjoy many political and civil rights and aspire to greater constitutional freedom. The German Democratic Republic, the People's Republic of China, and the Democratic People's Republic of Korea are drab despotisms, inspired by vulgar Marxist-Leninist ideology.

Logic seemingly would suggest that the high principle of national self-determination should be applied to these divided countries, as to all others. But merely to assert the principle skirts crucial questions. Who shall be the agent of reunification? What shall be the means of reunification—war or free popular elections? Who shall dominate the unified state? How shall the unified state relate to a world divided between free and totalitarian systems?

An instructive example is the dark fate of another once-divided but now unified country—Vietnam. A drama of political purification is being enacted in South Vietnam as it was enacted earlier in North Vietnam, North Korea, mainland China, and the Soviet Union. "Non-progressive," "reactionary," "imperialist," "bourgeois" categories of persons are being liquidated; the police state exterminates the enemies of the "people," or hauls them off to concentration camps. The relentless totalitarian mentality finally got its way.

Americans have been kind to some Vietnamese who managed to escape this frightening catastrophe—those who fled to the open seas in small boats. Civic groups and relief organizations have rallied to help them, with characteristic American good will. But it troubles our conscience to admit that this gruesome consequence of "reunification" and "national liberation" was the outcome of a test of wills in which ours came in second.

The Barrier to Reunification

In an important sense, the United States has long been the chief force in preventing the "final solution" of Chinese and Korean unity. From the 1950s to the 1970s, Taiwan and South Korea both were client states, protected by legally binding security guarantees and a physical military presence. Both governments, like their totalitarian counterparts, have long claimed to be repositories of their "nation"; they have aspired to the goal of unity, as have their opposites. The presence of U.S. power has constrained these hopes. It is not, and has not been, a purpose of American foreign policy to use these clients as agents for the forcible reunification of their countries. It never was U.S. policy to "liberate" mainland China or North Korea; the United States in each case forswore such a strategy. But America's Communist adversaries have not reciprocated. Without an American guarantee, Taiwan and South Korea would have been "liberated" years ago; the two Chinas and the two Koreas would now be effectively and tragically united, as the two Vietnams are now united.

The totalitarians have continued to endorse the use of force as a way of imposing their will. The tunnels tirelessly dug under the Demilitarized Zone between North and South Korea were (and perhaps still are) intended to provide a subterranean channel for surprise invasion. Despite deep differences between the Soviet Union and the People's Republic of China, in principle they both support Kim Il-sung's plan to unify Korea, by force if necessary. Moscow and Peking continue publicly to demand the withdrawal of U.S. troops from the South. While a renewed war in the Korean peninsula may be something that neither rival now wishes, their competition for Pyongyang's fealty gives the North Koreans a freedom of maneuver that poses a major danger in Asia today.

Similarly, the current leadership of the People's Republic has by no means forsworn the use of force as a means of annexing Taiwan. To Peking, thanks in part to U.S. diplomatic concessions, the Taiwan problem is a "domestic matter"; Washington under Carter, and before him Nixon, conceded the logic of Peking's case. For Peking, the gathering-in of Taiwan is only a matter of time, and it would prefer to settle the matter in the 1980s.

'What's Mine Is Mine . . .'

In dealing with Taiwan and Korea, as with Vietnam, the U.S. State Department has long pressed for compromise. Not so our adversaries. For them, as one Sovietologist has expressed it, "what's mine is mine; what's yours is negotiable."

Yet Washington continues to hope for mutually acceptable compromise—in effect, "what's mine is mine and what's yours is yours." One such hope, never clearly articulated by Washington, was for a two-China policy and a two-Korea policy (just as there once was a two-Vietnam policy). Under such an arrangement, each part would accept and recognize the other's existence: the two would agree to deal pragmatically with each other. Each would gain U.N. membership and general diplomatic acceptance, and the live-and-let-live compromise would be blessed by the Great Powers. Such a formula would closely resemble the "German solution."

Washington lost the two-China option in 1972 when President Nixon accepted the Shanghai Communiqué—the "one China" principle. This agreement paved the way for the breaking of diplomatic relations with Taiwan in December 1978.

The two-state principle on the East Asian mainland survives only in Korea. Here U.S. diplomacy trudges along, hoping that some day the adversaries will come to their senses and acknowledge how reasonable our proposals have always been.

The past three decades have seen economic and social miracles in Taiwan and South Korea. In the early 1950s, both were backward, impoverished, largely peasant societies. Korea was in ruins. Each is now a prosperous, vigorous part of the Pacific-basin economy. Both enjoy economic growth rates far exceeding those of the Western democracies—to say nothing of the growth rates of their Communist neighbors. Their people see affluence on the horizon.

Taiwan has a sound balance of growth between its industrial and agricultural sectors. One of Asia's most densely populated lands, it currently is also Asia's chief food-exporting country, thereby confounding Malthusian theory. Its total foreign trade annually exceeds that of the Chinese mainland. South Korean economic achievements are equally impressive. In 1945, when Korea was first divided, the North was the industrialized part, the South a backward rural society; the Japanese, during their forty-year rule of the peninsula (1905-45), had concentrated their investments in the North. Today the South's industrial economy towers over that of the North. South Korean industrial exports are marketed around the world. So skilled are South Korea's engineers that large numbers of them are engaged in major development projects in Saudi Arabia and other Persian Gulf states. Korean automobiles now successfully compete with Japanese ones in European markets.

Students of Third World economic growth (or stagnation) typically ignore these achievements. For instance, the Independent Commission on International Development Issues in February 1980 issued its well-publicized Brandt Report, which asserted that Third World poverty was due to exploitation by wealthy Western countries, the United States in particular. Only twelve lines of the report were devoted to the economic accomplishments of Taiwan, South Korea, Malaysia, Singapore, and Hong Kong: they were said to have been able "to take advantage of the international division of labor in highly competitive world markets . . ." (see Peter Day, "Beneath Charity: The Brandt Report," *Policy Review*, Summer 1980, p. 86).

Since the early 1960s, neither Korea nor Taiwan has been a supplicant for international handouts or for foreign humanitarian aid. Each has been eager to attract private foreign investment by creating a hospitable climate for it; each has offered positive incentives to Western and Japanese business firms. Their "export processing zones"—in which foreign firms establish plants under remarkably attractive contractual arrangements—are so successful that other Asian and African states (notably India, South Africa, Liberia, and the Philippines) are now emulating them. Neither government has whipped up populistic resentment against "imperialist exploiters," and in neither case has there been a looming threat of nationalization. Both have rejected socialist state planning and control; hence their economies contrast dramatically with the lethargic, regressive socialist economy that is typical of Third World states.

Some observers of these two singular success stories dismiss their importance: after all, it is said, both these half-countries enjoyed the benefits of Japanese economic tutelage for nearly half a century. But this is sophistry; many other Third World countries experienced decades if not whole centuries of Western economic tutelage and investment before gaining independence—Indonesia being a pertinent example.

Linear extrapolations make bad prophecy, especially now, with the great uncertainties about world trade prompted by the energy crisis. As of late 1980, the South Korean economy (though not Taiwan's), after a period of intense industrial growth, was experiencing a deep recession, particularly in its automotive and electronics industries. But if Taiwan and South Korea maintain some of their pace in economic growth, their living standards may soon rival those of many Western advanced industrial societies, as do Singapore's today. Each in its way is already a mini-Japan, seeking a place in the forefront of technological progress.

The Burden of Defense

These two economic miracles have occurred under a constant threat of hostile attack. Without an American defense guarantee, neither Taiwan nor Korea could possibly have been thought by foreign investors and businessmen to have a safe and hospitable climate. Unlike Japan, each has been burdened by heavy defense expenditures, including a large standing army. So advanced are

Taiwan and South Korea today that they both have the capacity to "go nuclear," a temptation to which they may yield if they are abandoned by friends.

Both Taiwan and South Korea are authoritarian states. The Republic of China is governed by a one-party system. The Republic of Korea has oscillated between civilian and military rule. After the assassination of President Park in 1979, the military were in power. Now civilian authority has again been installed. The quest for a viable constitutional regime continues, however, its prospects problematical.

Americans seeking to sponsor human rights in other people's countries draw frequent attention to specific violations in both Taiwan and South Korea. But some seem to apply a double standard to human rights in East Asia. In 1976, for instance, Congressman Don Fraser's subcommittee on international organizations of the House Foreign Affairs Committee spent weeks taking testimony about rights infringement in South Korea. Only at the insistence of outsiders did it finally agree to spend one day, in pro forma fashion, listening to sketchy descriptions of the situation in North Korea, where human rights are non-existent. Washington has been virtually silent about rights violations in mainland China; by contrast, even after Washington's diplomatic break with Taiwan the Carter State Department chided the Republic of China for supposedly harsh sentences of Formosa nationalists who were on trial for instigating a riot.

In contrast to their totalitarian counterparts, both Taiwan and the Republic of Korea are in many respects quite open societies. The press, though far from free on domestic political subjects, gives fairly straight coverage to foreign news (as is true in most authoritarian countries). Koreans and Taiwanese can easily learn about the world around them. They can move around their countries freely and change jobs. They can own property. Their rights to religious worship, whether Christian, Buddhist, or Confucian, are not constrained. Universities and research institutes enjoy wide freedoms.

In both countries, and for understandable reasons, it is sometimes impossible to distinguish those police measures taken for genuine security reasons from those motivated by the regime's desire to curtail the legitimate activities of its political foes. Yet in each the limits on civil or political rights are those of an authoritarian, partly free state. Political behavior in the two states is affected by the pervasive influences of the Free World, to which each has long been intimately linked.

The Carter Asian Policy

The signs of inconsistency in U.S. policy toward Taiwan and South Korea in the 1970s increased with the advent of the Carter administration. Both Nixon and Ford, as each played the China card, had reaffirmed U.S. intentions to protect Taiwan and Korea from armed attack—even as they conceded to Peking that the Taiwan issue was one to be settled by the Chinese themselves. With Carter, however, came a new foreign-policy establishment that included strange bedfellows: former anti-war activists; chastened former officials deeply affected by traumas of the Vietnam War who now doubted America's role as an active hegemonic power; anti-Soviet *Realpolitikers* who viewed East Asian politics as peripheral to the Washington-Peking-Moscow triangle; Sinophiles anxious to end the three-decade breach between America and China. And then Carter himself, a president singularly inexperienced in world affairs.

Washington's December 1978 decision to break diplomatic and security ties with the Republic of China sent tremors throughout East Asia; seen in conjunction with Carter's announced plan to phase U.S. troops out of Korea, it clearly foreshadowed fundamental changes in the region.

Carter's general view of the East Asian strategic situation arose in part from a genuine fear of involvement in a third war on the Asian mainland. The decisions to withdraw 20,000 ground troops from Korea and to normalize relations with the People's Republic of China were widely perceived as unilateral gestures that won no concessions, and as a strategic retreat. The troop withdrawals would, Carter said, be synchronized with improvements in South Korea's own fighting units. Furthermore, U.S. air power would remain as a guarantee, and of course the doughty Seventh Fleet would stay around. But the promise of continuing air cover recalls one of Aesop's fables: when the Eagle proposed an alliance with the Lion, the Lion replied, "How can I trust anyone as a friend who is able to fly away from his obligation whenever he pleases?" And it appears that Carter from the outset had decided to abandon Taiwan totally if Peking insisted on it.

There is a heavy price to be paid for abandoning allies, and the price is even greater when new concessions follow on the heels of a major abandonment like that in Vietnam. Ally, friend, and neutral alike were shaken by a perceived decline in America's willingness to keep its commitments. Even adversary governments were apprehensive. If what Peking wanted was a sturdy, dependable ally, it must have had its doubts about the United States, whose abject abandonment of traditional allies—for few solid gains—made it appear as a thrice-faithless partner now pledging fidelity to a fourth. Peking must also have wondered whether the U.S. abandonment of Taiwan and threatened retreat from South Korea were part of a larger pattern of U.S. disengagement from the region as a whole—something Peking greatly feared.

From the Japanese perspective, U.S. disengagement from these two countries could only be seen as a new threat to Japanese security and perhaps a harbinger of the abandonment of Japan. Such fears were reinforced by a 1978 book co-edited by a prominent Carter administration adviser on East Asia in which it was observed: "In gradually shifting to the Japanese responsibility for defending their own interests, the United States would extricate itself from its leading role in an area of secondary importance to American security" (Michael Oksenberg and Robert B. Oxnam, eds., *Dragon and Eagle: United States–China Relations*, p. 301).

In the joint communiqué on normalization (January 1, 1979; the text appears as Appendix B of this study), the United States agreed to recognize the "Government of the People's Republic of China as the sole legal government of China." The United States once more affirmed Peking's position that "there is but one China and Taiwan is part of China." Washington notified Taipei that it was "terminating" diplomatic relations and also the treaty between the

United States and the Republic of China. It would, of course, continue to have an "interest in the peaceful resolution of the Taiwan issue and expects that the Taiwan issue will be settled peacefully by the Chinese themselves"—a statement hardly in harmony with Peking's own frigid announcement that the means it would choose to bring Taiwan "back into the embrace of the motherland . . . is China's internal affair."

Unofficial Diplomacy in Taipei

What remained of the tattered U.S.-Taiwan connection? When the diplomatic break was announced, the White House pledged to continue relations with the *people* of Taiwan, on an "unofficial basis"; there would be an American Institute, a non-profit organization through which "unofficial" contacts could be maintained. As it turned out, this institute is a fascinating hybrid in the diplomatic world. Patterned after the Japanese office established in Taipei when Tokyo broke formal relations with the Republic of China, it is an embassy in all but name. The Peking authorities seem able to live with it. Despite clamors among some American conservatives to see full diplomatic relations restored, this institute and its Taiwan equivalent in Washington are more than adequate for workable bilateral relations.

The whole Peking-U.S.-Taiwan issue saw a fascinating switch of executive and congressional attitudes in the United States. Scarcely five years before, it was Congress that pressed for U.S. withdrawals from Asia, while the executive branch dug its heels in. In 1979, however, the White House had hardly bared the somber details of its accord with Peking when powerful congressional opposition to the abandonment of Taiwan arose. The Taiwan Relations bill submitted to Congress by the administration was subsequently amended by Congress in such a way as virtually to restore former U.S. commitments to Taiwan. Senator Frank Church, then chairman of the Senate Foreign Relations Committee, criticized the White House bill as "woefully inadequate" and emphasized the importance the United States should attach to the "future security and well-being of the people of Taiwan" (quoted in Edward K. Snyder, A. James Gregor, and Maria Hsia Chang, *The Taiwan Relations Act and the Defense of the Republic of China* [Berkeley: Institute of International Studies, University of California, 1980], p. 17). In deference to White House wishes, the Taiwan bill had made no reference to Taiwan's security; as amended and enacted, the bill—now law—contains language that serves as a surrogate for the defense treaty that Carter abrogated. The key provisions of the bill signed by Carter into law are:

> SEC. 2(b). It is the policy of the United States ... (4) to consider any effort to determine the future of Taiwan by other than peaceful means, including by boycotts or embargoes, a threat to the peace and security of the Western Pacific and of grave concern to the United States; (5) to provide Taiwan with arms of a defensive character; and (6) to maintain the capacity of the United States to resist any resort to force or other forms of coercion that should jeopardize the security, or social or economic system, of the people on Taiwan.
>
> SEC. 3(1) In furtherance of the policy set forth in section 2 of this Act, the United States will make available to Taiwan such defense articles and defense services in such quantity as may be necessary to enable Taiwan to maintain a sufficient self-defense capability [Public Law 96-8, April 10, 1979, 96th Congress, 93 Stat. 14; for the full text of the act see Appendix C].

This leaves us in a twilight zone of diplomatic ambiguity. The Taiwan Relations Act has not evoked outrage in Peking. The Chinese Communist leaders obviously have far more pressing concerns at present than the "liberation" of Taiwan. By now they must know that any forceful move against Taiwan, whether economic sanctions, a blockade, or an actual military attack, would incur extremely high and unacceptable risks, particularly to its new and valued relations with Japan, the West, and most of all the United States.

American interests were greatly harmed by the indecisiveness and unpredictability of American behavior toward Taiwan during 1979 and 1980. In Washington, Taiwan as a sovereign entity both existed and did not exist. Its integrity was affirmed by congressional statute while it was studiously ignored in administration rhetoric. Responsibility for its safety was repudiated by the executive branch and reaffirmed by Congress.

One constant in the strange situation is Peking's unrelenting will, tempered now by necessary patience. That will contrasts with a temperamental American inability to wait, and a preference for quick solutions.

One test of Washington's intentions will be its evolving policy toward selling arms to Taiwan for its defense needs. The United States needs to show the world that it will stand by its allies and friends even as out of necessity it develops a closer relationship with a former (and potential) enemy.

Soviet Buildup in the Pacific

While the Soviet divisions deployed along the Sino-Soviet border have remained constant in number over the past few years, they have been upgraded, as have the supporting air forces; this upgrading has proceeded at the same pace as that of the comparable units facing NATO countries. More ominous is the impressive buildup in Soviet military forces oriented toward Japan and the Pacific generally. One example is the increase in ground forces deployed in the Soviet Pacific regions, including the island of Sakhalin and the southern Kuril Islands. A second is the positioning of modern, extended-range nuclear weapons systems (the SS-20 surface-to-surface missile system and the Backfire bomber, which have caused such consternation in Western European circles). Third—and most important of all—is the steady augmentation of the capability and reach of the Soviet Pacific fleet, which now boasts twice the tonnage of the U.S. Seventh Fleet and has many more surface combat vessels. Supported by a large merchant marine and fishing fleet—both under naval command and performing a wide range of military support missions—that fleet poses an explicit challenge to control of the Western Pacific, on which the free nations of East Asia utterly depend for their survival in peace and in war.

The growth of Soviet military power in northeast Asia has been paralleled by the growth of North Korea's military power. For at least ten years North Korea has devoted an extraordinarily large share of its national resources, generally estimated at 15-20 per cent of the GNP, to its armed forces. The size and stance of these forces combined with the North's expansionist policy make the Korean peninsula the most dangerous area in the region, if not the world.

While the North Korean buildup has been going on for a decade, only recently has enough intelligence collection and analysis been done to measure it accurately. The 1980 U.S. Department of Defense estimate of ground forces strength is 600,000—more than 100,000 above the 1978 estimate. Correspondingly, combat division totals have been increased from 25 to about 40, tanks from 1,950 to 2,600, field artillery pieces from 3,000 to nearly 4,000, and so on. Numbers by themselves are inconclusive. What counts is that the North outguns South Korea by every measurement of ready military power. Even if the North Korean buildup leveled off—which it shows no sign of doing—there is no way South Korea could catch up in the foreseeable future.

Other aspects of North Korea's military machine are even more disturbing. Most of the combat units are deployed in the areas closest to the South. They are protected by a virtually impenetrable counterintelligence screen and are thus capable of launching a massive invasion with little or no warning. Mechanization grows, increasing the army's capacity for rapid advance into the South Korean heartland (Seoul is only twenty-five miles from the provisional boundary). Notably, too, the North Korean army structure includes the world's largest commando formation, possibly numbering 80-100,000; these elite troops are reliably reported to have the mission of infiltrating the South by a variety of means (air, sea, overland, or through tunnels), either in conjunction with the regular forces or separately, to cause disruption and sow confusion in rear areas. The armed forces are supported by a defense-industrial base that produces, in quantity, all needed equipment except aircraft and sophisticated missiles. Moreover, an enormous amount of money and labor has been used to provide bomb-proof facilities (mainly underground) for first-line aircraft and their support, for stocks of supplies essential for combat, and for selected defense industries; North Korea thus resembles an armadillo, invulnerable to air attack by conventional weapons.

The North Korean armed forces, far exceeding the legitimate needs of self-defense, are an unmistakable sign of the regime's aggressive design to unify the peninsula under Communist aegis. There is no evidence that Peking or Moscow would give either tacit assent or encouragement to any North Korean action against the South. But this xenophobic state is no longer under their precise control, and Kim Il-sung's freedom of action is greatly enhanced by the rift between the two Communist powers.

From a strategic standpoint, both Taiwanese and South Korean security depend on domestic cohesion in the face of external or internal attempts to destabilize their governments and societies. Unrest is a far greater danger in South Korea than in Taiwan. The Peking authorities, for obvious reasons, are wary of upheavals fomented by "Formosan" nationalists; these movements encourage tendencies toward a separatist Taiwanese state that might explicitly repudiate a national connection with China. Not so in Korea. Civil unrest there, whatever its origins, would gravely weaken the republic without causing a rejection of the nationality principle. If South Korea's military were turned inward to deal with a major domestic crisis, U.S. ground forces would be in an embarrassing position. Furthermore, while a military solution of the Taiwanese problem from Peking's standpoint is currently out of the question, a similar solution of the Korean one certainly is not. Pyongyang has but one strategic front; Peking, were it to launch a "liberation" of Taiwan, would have two to worry about.

These dangers are facts of life for the South Koreans and Taiwanese, who long have lived in jeopardy. Americans know such experiences only vicariously. Many of us regard defense as a luxury, danger either as something of our own making or as an illusion. During the Senate hearings on his nomination as secretary of state (1949), Dean Acheson pointed to the moral necessity of facing unpleasant realities:

> The judgment of nature upon error is death.... The future is unpredictable. Only one thing—the unexpected—can be reasonably expected.... The part of wisdom is to be prepared for what may happen, rather than base our course upon faith in what should happen.... Here you can be wrong only once.

CHAPTER EIGHT

Toward a Security Community

Do not wait for extraordinary circumstances to do good; try to use ordinary situations.
JOHANN RICHTER (1763-1825)

Circumstances!—I make circumstances!
NAPOLEON BONAPARTE (1769-1821)

FOR YEARS SOME PEOPLE have been saying that America's destiny lies in the Pacific region, that the Pacific basin is the future nexus of the free world's economy, and that the peaceful interdependence of states in this region is essential to America's wellbeing. While the economic evidence for these assertions grows more impressive each year, this evidence is not reflected in the way Americans rank political problems in the world.

Humanitarian liberals see the north-south issue—the "rich-poor" antithesis—as America's principal challenge. Hawks and doves argue about the strategic balance largely in East-West terms; *Realpolitik* practitioners perceive the growing Soviet threat chiefly in the crucible of Europe and the Middle East; the Persian Gulf energy issue is seen as one primarily affecting the solidarity of the Western alliance. Our sense of security seems scarcely affected by our Pacific connections.

At home, our multi-ethnic difficulties since the mid-1950s have not really included Asians; the political agenda as set by activists focuses almost exclusively on blacks, Hispanics, and American

Indians. Chinese, Japanese, Koreans, and Vietnamese have easily and rapidly moved into the mainstream of American life without militancy or privilege-seeking. Few Asian-Americans, climbing the social and economic ladder, have demanded preferences, quotas, federal welfare assistance, or invidious linguistic favors. Few have shown much interest in seeking preferential U.S. policies toward the Pacific

But American culture has had a singularly powerful impact on the Pacific region. While traditional cultures still flourish, the dominant political cultures in non-Communist East Asia have been Westernized and Americanized to a degree that would have been unimaginable half a century ago.

The Peaceful Pacific

Thanks to the U.S. presence, for the past three decades the islands of East Asia have been spared the horrors of war that afflicted the mainland. Since 1945 the Pacific has taken on what General Douglas MacArthur years ago called the "friendly aspect of a peaceful lake." America's unchallenged role along that island chain stretching from the Aleutians to the Philippines has provided an overarching order for these insular states and South Korea, as well as the strategic rim of a vast moat for America's own security. And for the time being, good fortune has granted us a condition of bipolarity on the northeast Asia totalitarian mainland, rather than its domination by one hostile power.

After a decade of doubt, the U.S. presence in East Asia seems more certain than at any time since the Vietnam War. Very few Americans, and no significant political figures, today argue the case for withdrawal from East Asia.

So the U.S. retreat across the Pacific has not materialized. Our security ties with South Korea have been reaffirmed; this was done with particular firmness in 1980 when civil disturbances in South Korea might well have tempted Kim Il-sung to increase subversive intervention. Our defense collaboration with Japan is one of growing mutual respect, reciprocity, and coordination. Congress on its own initiative has established by law a sound basis for new security relationships with Taiwan. In 1979, U.S. base rights in the Philippines were satisfactorily renewed. And the diplomatic and political climate between America and its East Asian allies today is more trustworthy than it was in the first two years of the Carter administration. As of late 1980, ignoble threats of American abandonment had ceased, in large measure because of the refusal of many persons inside and outside the Carter administration to countenance them.

So much for the good news; now for the bad.

The most serious threats to the region remain the Sino-Soviet rivalry and Soviet expansionism. Some U.S. Defense Department optimists have welcomed this rivalry as a condition that would turn the aggressive tendencies of the two Communist giants inward, away from the non-Communist world. But it has not had that effect. The conflict also erupts outward, as each seeks to check its rival by using force in adjacent areas. The Sino-Soviet conflict rages, by proxy, along and across the Thai border, and it threatens nearby Malaysia as well. A major renewal of fighting along the Chinese-Vietnamese border threatens the security of nations in the region by heightening Sino-Soviet tensions there. The rivalry also adversely affects the fragile balance in the Korean peninsula by enhancing the independence of Kim Il-sung. The Soviet strategy of encircling China cannot be distinguished, except analytically, from the general tendencies of Soviet expansion that are detrimental to the security of America's non-Communist allies.

The second serious threat is the impact on the global balance of power of the Soviet strategic buildup in East Asia. To see this steady increase as merely an aspect of the Sino-Soviet contest would be a serious mistake; it is a part of the growth of Soviet power in general. To be sure, Russia was an East Asian power long before the 1917 revolution. The difference now is that Moscow is rapidly becoming a major *Pacific* power.

The United States confronted no serious naval rival in the Pacific in the three decades following World War II. Now, however, the U.S. Seventh Fleet—severely reduced in numbers, charged with a dual mission in East Asia and in the Persian Gulf, and hobbled by obsolescence and morale problems—faces a huge, growing, self-confident new rival. Moscow now fully uses the U.S.-built Cam Ranh Bay base in Vietnam. It has become a naval power even in Southeast Asia.

Principles for a Security Community

There is no accepted U.S. "doctrine" to shape our strategic thinking about East Asia today. Given the circumstances, this may be all to the good; doctrines easily get out of hand and live a life of their own as masters rather than servants. Yet performance should be informed by some governing principles. I offer the following as principles for enhancing security in the Western Pacific:

1. The security of the non-Communist states should become more a mutual responsibility. Until now, U.S. security arrangements in Asia have been bilateral; the United States, always the dominant partner, has borne the chief burden of defense. This pattern no longer reflects reality. The states in the region should play a far greater role in their own defense. Such cooperation probably should not now take the form of a collective security pact, which could give rise to unnecessary apprehensions. It should instead be in the form of a security *community*, united by a common, even instinctive perception of shared vital interests.

2. Japan in particular must play a far greater strategic role, especially in maritime defense. The only realistic way for this to be accomplished today, given Japanese domestic politics and the politics of the Pacific, is for Tokyo's role to evolve and be exercised within an informal concert of friendly, non-Communist countries in and near the region. As with German rearmament in the 1950s, such defense growth must be disciplined by the constraints of a comprehensive—if informal—security system in which strategic planning is dedicated to the security of all members. Although there is today little prospect that Japan might again become a "rogue elephant" in the region, the Japanese people and the world both need reassurance that a Japan strategically active is a Japan constrained by mutual obligations.

3. Such a community need not be contractual, but the responsibilities of each member should be clear. America's security

partners in East Asia would therefore be on this side of the iron and bamboo curtains; they could include Australia, New Zealand, Indonesia, the Philippines, Singapore, Malaysia, Taiwan (informally), Japan, and South Korea. The chief mission of such a community should be to protect the tranquillity of the Western Pacific. The principal challenge should be to cope with the spread of Soviet power and the danger that this power poses to the vital maritime lanes of the region. The core of this security community should be South Korea, Japan, and Taiwan. A militarily strong Taiwan, if not explicitly included in such arrangements, remains nevertheless a key element in the security of Japan. It should be an unswerving object of American policy to see that Taiwan receives military equipment sufficient to its own defense, however much Peking or Moscow may object.

4. These Pacific security arrangements should emerge organically. They cannot be brought about by proclamation from Washington; the days when U.S. secretaries of state made momentous commencement-day speeches and foreign ministers of friendly countries scurried to respond are now over. It will be some time before the United States fully regains its reputation of leadership. Anyway, the U.S. role in the Pacific could not and should not resemble what it was in the 1950s.

5. A major goal for such a Pacific community should be to reduce greatly the unfortunate dependence on what I have called the "China crutch" (see chapter 4). Over-reliance on China for East Asian security entails the risk of increasing regional tensions; China's interests are China's interests. The Pacific collective security recommended here would in no way threaten China's vital interests but *would* serve as a deterrent to Chinese adventurism. A Pacific community can exist side-by-side with China. This would mean that the non-totalitarian states of East Asia would not have to choose fatalistically between two totalitarian giants. Reduced dependence on the China crutch, moreover, would serve to reassure Moscow that the Pacific community has no interest in increasing Sino-Soviet tensions.

6. The chief motivating force of such a community should be, not anti-Communism as such, but the development and security of

free and independent states with responsible, responsive governments. It is certainly true that in the 1970s a growing fear of U.S. abandonment contributed to the increasing authoritarian character of some East Asian countries, notably South Korea and the Philippines. Full human rights are the final fruit of confident peoples; they may wither under the insecurity of external threats. The interests of democracy in the Pacific region are directly related to the perception of external and internal threats.

7. A Pacific community along these lines would be buttressed by its own economic dynamism. Such a combination of military, political, and economic strength could have a positive impact on political developments on the Communist mainland.

I cannot overstress the idea of constant organic growth, as opposed to mechanical contrivance. Many informal, positive steps have already been taken. There are already intimate ties between Japan and Australia, between Australia and Malaysia, and between U.S. naval forces and those of all the insular states. It is possible to play in concert without a conspicuous conductor as long as everyone knows the score.

Such a Pacific security community is impossible without the presence of the United States as an active partner. It can therefore be possible only when the United States once more is morally committed and militarily able to respond to the ominous growth of Soviet military power, not only in East Asia but throughout the world. Only Americans can make that choice.

APPENDIX A

The Shanghai Communiqué
February 27, 1972

President Richard Nixon made a historic trip to the People's Republic of China in February 1972 and met with Chou En-lai and Mao Tse-tung. The joint statement issued at the close of the visit revealed that, though there was some similarity of interests between the two countries, many differences remained.

PRESIDENT RICHARD NIXON OF THE United States of America visited the People's Republic of China at the invitation of Premier Chou En-lai of the People's Republic of China from February 21 to February 28, 1972. Accompanying the President were Mrs. Nixon, U.S. Secretary of State William Rogers, Assistant to the President Dr. Henry Kissinger, and other American officials.

President Nixon met with Chairman Mao Tse-tung of the Communist Party of China on February 21. The two leaders had a serious and frank exchange of views on Sino-U.S. relations and world affairs.

During the visit, extensive, earnest and frank discussions were held between President Nixon and Premier Chou En-lai on the normalization of relations between the United States of America and the People's Republic of China, as well as on other matters of interest to both sides. In addition, Secretary of State William Rogers and Foreign Minister Chi Peng-fei held talks in the same spirit.

President Nixon and his party visited Peking and viewed cultural, industrial, and agricultural sites, and they also toured Hangchow and Shanghai, where, continuing discussions with Chinese leaders, they viewed similar places of interest.

The leaders of the People's Republic of China and the United States of America found it beneficial to have this opportunity, after so many years without contact, to present candidly to one another their views on a variety of issues. They reviewed the international situation in which important changes and great upheavals are taking place and expounded their respective positions and attitudes.

The U.S. side stated: Peace in Asia and peace in the world requires efforts both to reduce immediate tensions and to eliminate the basic causes of conflict. The United States will work for a just and secure peace: just, because it fulfills the aspirations of peoples and nations for freedom and progress; secure, because it removes the danger of foreign aggression. The United States supports individual freedom and social progress for all the peoples of the world, free of outside pressure or intervention. The United States believes that the effort to reduce tensions is served by improving communication between countries that have different ideologies so as to lessen the risks of confrontation through accident, miscalculation, or misunderstanding. Countries should treat each other with mutual respect and be willing to compete peacefully, letting performance be the ultimate judge. No country should claim infallibility, and each country should be prepared to re-examine its own attitudes for the common good. The United States stressed that the peoples of Indochina should be allowed to determine their destiny without outside intervention; its constant primary objective has been a negotiated solution; the eight-point proposal put forward by the Republic of Vietnam and the United States on January 27, 1972, represents a basis for the attainment of that objective; in the absence of a negotiated settlement the United States envisages the ultimate withdrawal of all U.S. forces from the region consistent with the aim of self-determination for each country of Indochina. The United States will maintain its close ties with and support for the Republic of Korea; the United States will support efforts of the Republic of Korea to seek a relaxation of tension and increased communication in the Korean peninsula. The United States places the highest value on its friendly relations with Japan; it will continue to develop the existing close bonds. Consistent with the United Nations Security Council Resolution of December 21, 1971, the United States favors the continuation of the ceasefire between India and Pakistan and the withdrawal of all military forces to within their own territories and to their own sides of the ceasefire line in Jammu and Kashmir; the United States supports the right of the peoples of South Asia to shape their own future in peace, free of military threat, and without having the area become the subject of great power rivalry.

The Chinese side stated: Wherever there is oppression, there is resistance. Countries want independence, nations want liberation, and the people want revolution—this has become the irresistible trend of history. All nations, big or small, should be equal; big nations should not bully the small and strong nations should not bully the weak. China will never be a superpower, and it opposes hegemony and power politics of any kind. The Chinese side stated that it firmly supports the struggles of all the oppressed people and nations for freedom and liberation and that the people of all countries have the right to choose their social systems according to their own wishes and the right to safeguard the independence, sovereignty, and territorial integrity of their own countries and oppose foreign aggression, interference, control, and subversion. All foreign troops should be withdrawn to their own countries.

The Chinese side expressed its firm support to the peoples of Vietnam, Laos, and Cambodia in their efforts for the attainment of their goal and its firm support to the seven-point proposal of the Provisional Revolutionary Government of the Republic of South Vietnam and the elaboration of February this year on the two key problems in the proposal, and to the Joint Declaration of the Summit Conference of the Indochinese Peoples. It firmly supports the eight-point program for the peaceful unification of Korea put forward by the Government of the Democratic People's Republic of Korea on April 12, 1971, and the stand for the abolition of the "U.N. Commission for the Unification and Rehabilitation of

Korea." It firmly opposes the revival and outward expansion of Japanese militarism and firmly supports the Japanese people's desire to build an independent, democratic, peaceful, and neutral Japan. It firmly maintains that India and Pakistan should, in accordance with the United Nations resolutions on the India-Pakistan question, immediately withdraw all their forces to their respective territories and to their own sides of the ceasefire line in Jammu and Kashmir and firmly supports the Pakistan Government and people in their struggle to preserve their independence and sovereignty and the people of Jammu and Kashmir in their struggle for the right of self-determination.

There are essential differences between China and the United States in their social systems and foreign policies. However, the two sides agreed that countries, regardless of their social systems, should conduct their relations on the principles of respect for the sovereignty and territorial integrity of all states, non-aggression against other states, non-interference in the internal affairs of other states, equality and mutual benefit, and peaceful coexistence. International disputes should be settled on this basis, without resorting to the use or threat of force. The United States and the People's Republic of China are prepared to apply these principles to their mutual relations.

With these principles of international relations in mind the two sides stated that:

—progress toward the normalization of relations between China and the United States is in the interest of all countries;

—both wish to reduce the danger of international military conflict;

—neither should seek hegemony in the Asia-Pacific region and each is opposed to efforts by any other country or group of countries to establish such hegemony; and

—neither is prepared to negotiate on behalf of any third party or to enter into agreements or understandings with the other directed at other states.

Both sides are of the view that it would be against the interests of the peoples of the world for any major country to collude with another against other countries, or for major countries to divide up the world into spheres of interest.

The two sides reviewed the long-standing serious disputes between China and the United States. The Chinese side reaffirmed its position: The Taiwan question is the crucial question obstructing the normalization of relations between China and the United States; the Government of the People's Republic of China is the sole legal government of China; Taiwan is a province of China which has long been returned to the motherland; the liberation of Taiwan is China's internal affair in which no other country has the right to interfere; and all U.S. forces and military installations must be withdrawn from Taiwan. The Chinese Government firmly opposes any activities which aim at the creation of "one China, one Taiwan," "one China, two governments," "two Chinas," and "independent Taiwan" or advocate that "the status of Taiwan remains to be determined."

The U.S. side declared: The United States acknowledges that all Chinese on either side of the Taiwan Strait maintain there is but one China and that Taiwan is a part of China. The United States Government does not challenge that position. It reaffirms its interest in a peaceful settlement of the Taiwan question by the Chinese themselves. With this prospect in mind, it affirms the ultimate objective of the withdrawal of all U.S. forces and military installations from Taiwan. In the meantime, it will progressively reduce its force and military installations on Taiwan as the tension in the area diminishes.

The two sides agreed that it is desirable to broaden the understanding between the two peoples. To this end, they discussed specific areas in such fields as science, technology, culture, sports, and journalism, in which people-to-people contacts and exchanges would be mutually beneficial. Each side undertakes to facilitate the further development of such contacts and exchanges.

Both sides view bilateral trade as another area from which mutual benefit can be derived, and agreed that economic relations based on equality and mutual benefit are in the interest of the peoples of the two countries. They agree to facilitate the progressive development of trade between their two countries.

The two sides agreed that they will stay in contact through various channels, including the sending of a senior U.S. representative to Peking from time to time for concrete consultations to further the normalization of relations between the two countries and continue to exchange views on issues of common interest.

The two sides expressed the hope that the gains achieved during this visit would open up new prospects for the relations between the two countries. They believe that the normalization of relations between the two countries is not only in the interest of the Chinese and American peoples but also contributes to the relaxation of tension in Asia and the world.

President Nixon, Mrs. Nixon, and the American party expressed their appreciation for the gracious hospitality shown them by the Government and people of the People's Republic of China.

APPENDIX B

Joint Communiqué on the Establishment of Diplomatic Relations
The United States and the People's Republic of China, January 1, 1979

THE UNITED STATES OF AMERICA and the People's Republic of China have agreed to recognize each other and to establish diplomatic relations as of January 1, 1979.

The United States of America recognizes the Government of the People's Republic of China as the sole legal Government of China. Within this context, the people of the United States will maintain cultural, commercial and other unofficial relations with the people of Taiwan.

The United States of America and the People's Republic of China reaffirm the principles agreed on by the two sides in the Shanghai Communiqué and emphasize once again that:

- Both wish to reduce the danger of international military conflict.
- Neither should seek hegemony in the Asia-Pacific region or in any other region of the world and each is opposed to efforts by any other country or group of countries to establish such hegemony.
- Neither is prepared to negotiate on behalf of any third party or to enter into agreements or understandings with the other directed at other states.
- The United States of America acknowledges the Chinese position that there is but one China and Taiwan is part of China.
- Both believe that normalization of Sino-American relations is not only in the interest of the Chinese and American peoples but also contributes to the cause of peace in Asia and the world.

The United States of America and the People's Republic of China will exchange ambassadors and establish embassies on March 1, 1979.

APPENDIX C

Taiwan Relations Act
April 10, 1979

Soon after normalization of relations with the People's Republic of China was announced by President Jimmy Carter in December 1978, powerful opposition to the "abandonment" of Taiwan arose in Congress. The Taiwan Relations bill submitted by the administration was amended so that, as enacted into law (Public Law 96-8), it reaffirmed U.S. commitments to Taiwan.

AN ACT TO HELP MAINTAIN PEACE, security, and stability in the Western Pacific and to promote the foreign policy of the United States by authorizing the continuation of commercial, cultural, and other relations between the people of the United States and the people on Taiwan, and for other purposes.

SHORT TITLE

SECTION 1. This Act may be cited as the "Taiwan Relations Act."

FINDINGS AND DECLARATION OF POLICY

SEC. 2. (a) The President having terminated governmental relations between the United States and the governing authorities on Taiwan recognized by the United States as the Republic of China prior to January 1, 1979, the Congress finds that the enactment of this Act is necessary—

(1) to help maintain peace, security, and stability in the Western Pacific; and

(2) to promote the foreign policy of the United States by authorizing the continuation of commercial, cultural, and other relations between the people of the United States and the people on Taiwan.

(b) It is the policy of the United States—

(1) to preserve and promote extensive, close, and friendly commercial, cultural, and other relations between the people of the United States and the people on Taiwan, as well as the people on the China mainland and all other peoples of the Western Pacific area;

(2) to declare that peace and stability in the area are in the political, security, and economic interests of the United States, and are matters of international concern;

(3) to make clear that the United States decision to establish diplomatic relations with the People's Republic of China rests upon the expectation that the future of Taiwan will be determined by peaceful means;

(4) to consider any effort to determine the future of Taiwan by other than peaceful means, including by boycotts or embargoes, a threat to the peace and security of the Western Pacific area and of grave concern to the United States;

(5) to provide Taiwan with arms of a defensive character; and

(6) to maintain the capacity of the United States to resist any resort to force or other forms of coercion that would jeopardize the security, or the social or economic system, of the people on Taiwan.

(c) Nothing contained in this Act shall contravene the interest of the United States in human rights especially with respect to the human rights of all the approximately 18 million inhabitants of Taiwan. The preservation and enhancement of the human rights of all the people on Taiwan are hereby reaffirmed as objectives of the United States.

IMPLEMENTATION OF UNITED STATES POLICY WITH REGARD TO TAIWAN

SEC. 3. (a) In furtherance of the policy set forth in section 2 of this Act, the United States will make available to Taiwan such defense articles and defense services in such quantity as may be necessary to enable Taiwan to maintain a sufficient self-defense capability.

(b) The President and the Congress shall determine the nature and quantity of such defense articles and services based solely upon their judgment of the needs of Taiwan, in accordance with procedures established by law. Such determination of Taiwan's defense needs shall include review by United States military authorities in connection with recommendations to the President and the Congress.

(c) The President is directed to inform the Congress promptly of any threat to the security or the social or economic system of the people on Taiwan and any danger to the interests of the United States arising therefrom. The President and the Congress shall determine, in accordance with constitutional processes, appropriate action by the United States in response to any such danger.

APPLICATION OF LAWS; INTERNATIONAL AGREEMENTS

SEC. 4. (a) The absence of diplomatic relations or recognition shall not affect the application of the laws of the United States with respect to Taiwan, and the laws of the United States shall apply with respect to Taiwan in the manner that the laws of the United States applied with respect to Taiwan prior to January 1, 1979.

(b) The application of subsection (a) of this section shall include, but shall not be limited to, the following:

(1) Whenever the laws of the United States refer or relate to foreign countries, nations, states, governments, or similar entities, such terms shall include and such laws shall apply with respect to Taiwan.

(2) Whenever authorized by or pursuant to the laws of the United States to conduct or carry out programs, transactions, or other relations with respect to foreign countries, nations, states, governments, or similar entities, the President

or any agency of the United States Government is authorized to conduct and carry out, in accordance with section 6 of this Act, such programs, transactions, and other relations with respect to Taiwan (including, but not limited to, the performance of services for the United States through contracts with commercial entities on Taiwan), in accordance with the applicable laws of the United States.

(3)(A) The absence of diplomatic relations and recognition with respect to Taiwan shall not abrogate, infringe, modify, deny, or otherwise affect in any way any rights or obligations (including but not limited to those involving contracts, debts, or property interests of any kind) under the laws of the United States heretofore or hereafter required by or with respect to Taiwan.

(B) For all purposes under the laws of the United States, including actions in any court in the United States, recognition of the People's Republic of China shall not affect in any way the ownership of or other rights or interests in properties, tangible and intangible, and other things of value, owned or held on or prior to December 31, 1978, or thereafter acquired or earned by the governing authorities on Taiwan.

(4) Whenever the application of the laws of the United States depends upon the law that is or was applicable on Taiwan or compliance therewith, the law applied by the people on Taiwan shall be considered the applicable law for that purpose.

(5) Nothing in this Act, nor the facts of the President's action in extending diplomatic recognition to the People's Republic of China, the absence of diplomatic relations between the people on Taiwan and the United States, or the lack of recognition by the United States, and attendant circumstances thereto, shall be construed in any administrative or judicial proceeding as a basis for any United States Government agency, commission, or department to make a finding of fact or determination of law, under the Atomic Energy Act of 1954 and the Nuclear Non-Proliferation Act of 1978, to deny an export license application or to revoke an existing export license for nuclear exports to Taiwan.

(6) For the purposes of the Immigration and Nationality Act, Taiwan may be treated in the manner specified in the first sentence of section 202(b) of that Act.

(7) The capacity of Taiwan to sue and be sued in courts in the United States, in accordance with the laws of the United States, shall not be abrogated, infringed, modified, denied, or otherwise affected in any way by the absence of diplomatic relations or recognition.

(8) No requirement, whether expressed or implied, under the laws of the United States with respect to maintenance of diplomatic relations or recognition shall be applicable with respect to Taiwan.

(c) For all purposes, including actions in any court in the United States, the Congress approves the continuation in force of all treaties and other international agreements, including multilateral conventions, entered into by the United States and the governing authorities on Taiwan recognized by the United States as the Republic of China prior to January 1, 1979, and in force between them on December 31, 1978, unless and until terminated in accordance with law.

(d) Nothing in this Act may be construed as a basis for supporting the exclusion or expulsion of Taiwan from continued membership in any international financial institution or any other international organization.

OVERSEAS PRIVATE INVESTMENT CORPORATION

SEC. 5. (a) During the three-year period beginning on the date of enactment of this Act, the $1,000 per capita income restriction in clause (2) of the second undesignated paragraph of section 231 of the Foreign Assistance Act of 1961 shall not restrict the activities of the Overseas Private Investment Corporation in determining whether to provide any insurance, reinsurance, loans, or guaranties with respect to investment projects on Taiwan.

(b) Except as provided in subsection (a) of this section, in issuing insurance, reinsurance, loans, or guaranties with respect to investment projects on Taiwan, the Overseas Private Insurance Corporation shall apply the same criteria as those applicable in other parts of the world.

THE AMERICAN INSTITUTE OF TAIWAN

SEC. 6. (a) Programs, transactions, and other relations conducted or carried out by the President or any agency of the United States Government with respect to Taiwan shall, in the manner and to the extent directed by the President, be conducted and carried out by or through—

(1) The American Institute in Taiwan, a nonprofit corporation incorporated under the laws of the District of Columbia, or

(2) such comparable successor nongovernmental entity as the President may designate (hereafter in this Act referred to as the "Institute").

(b) Whenever the President or any agency of the United States Government is authorized or required by or pursuant to the laws of the United States to enter into, perform, enforce, or have in force an agreement or transaction relative to Taiwan, such agreement or transaction shall be entered into, performed, and enforced, in the manner and to the extent directed by the President, by or through the Institute.

(c) To the extent that any law, rule, regulation, or ordinance of the District of Columbia, or of any State or political subdivision thereof in which the Institute is incorporated or doing business, impedes or otherwise interferes with the performance of the functions of the Institute pursuant to this Act, such law, rule, regulation, or ordinance shall be deemed to be preempted by this Act.

SERVICES BY THE INSTITUTE TO UNITED STATES CITIZENS ON TAIWAN

SEC. 7. (a) The Institute may authorize any of its employees on Taiwan—

(1) to administer to or take from any person an oath, affirmation, affidavit, or deposition, and to perform any notarial act which any notary public is required or authorized by law to perform within the United States;

(2) to act as provisional conservator of the personal estates of deceased United States citizens; and

(3) to assist and protect the interests of United States persons by performing other acts such as are authorized to be performed outside the United States for consular purposes by such laws of the United States as the President may specify.

(b) Acts performed by authorized employees of the Institute under this section shall be valid, and of like force and effect within the United States, as if performed by any other person authorized under the laws of the United States to perform such acts.

TAX EXEMPT STATUS OF THE INSTITUTE

SEC. 8. (a) The Institute, its property, and its income are exempt from all taxation now or hereafter imposed by the United States (except to the extent that section 11(a)(3) of this Act requires the imposition of taxes imposed under Chapter 21 of the Internal Revenue Code of 1954, relating to the Federal Insurance Contributions Act) or by any State or local taxing authority of the United States.

(b) For purposes of the Internal Revenue Code of 1954, the Institute shall be treated as an organization described in sections 170(b)(1)(A), 170(c), 2055(a), 2106(a)(2)(A), 2522(a), and 2522(b).

FURNISHING PROPERTY AND SERVICES TO AND OBTAINING SERVICES FROM THE INSTITUTE

SEC. 9. (a) Any agency of the United States Government is authorized to sell, loan, or lease property (including interests therein) to, and to perform administrative and technical support functions and services for the operations of, the Institute upon such terms and conditions as the President may direct. Reimbursements to agencies under this subsection shall be credited to the current applicable appropriation of the agency concerned.

(b) Any agency of the United States Government is authorized to acquire and accept services from the Institute upon such terms and conditions as the President may direct. Whenever the President determines it to be in furtherance of the purposes of this Act, the procurement of services by such agencies from the Institute may be effected without regard to such laws of the United States normally applicable to the acquisition of services by such agencies as the President may specify by Executive order.

(c) Any agency of the United States Government making funds available to the Institute in accordance with this Act shall make arrangements with the Institute for the Comptroller General of the United States to have access to the books and records of the Institute and the opportunity to audit the operations of the Institute.

TAIWAN INSTRUMENTALITY

SEC. 10. (a) Whenever the President or any agency of the United States Government is authorized or required by or pursuant to the laws of the United

States to render or provide to or to receive or accept from Taiwan, any performance, communication, assurance, undertaking, or other action, such action shall, in the manner and to the extent directed by the President, be rendered or provided to, or received or accepted from, an instrumentality established by Taiwan which the President determines has the necessary authority under the laws applied by the people on Taiwan to provide assurances and take other actions on behalf of Taiwan in accordance with this Act.

(b) The President is requested to extend to the instrumentality established by Taiwan the same number of offices and complement of personnel as were previously operated in the United States by the governing authorities on Taiwan recognized as the Republic of China prior to January 1, 1979.

(c) Upon the granting by Taiwan of comparable privileges and immunities with respect to the Institute and its appropriate personnel, the President is authorized to extend with respect to the Taiwan instrumentality and its appropriate personnel, such privileges and immunities (subject to appropriate conditions and obligations) as may be necessary for the effective performance of their functions.

SEPARATION OF GOVERNMENT PERSONNEL FOR EMPLOYMENT WITH THE INSTITUTE

SEC. 11. (a)(1) Under such terms and conditions as the President may direct, any agency of the United States Government may separate from Government service for a specified period any officer or employee of that agency who accepts employment with the Institute.

(2) An officer or employee separated by an agency under paragraph (1) of this subsection for employment with the Institute shall be entitled upon termination of such employment to reemployment or reinstatement with such agency (or a successor agency) in an appropriate position with the attendant rights, privileges, and benefits which the officer or employee would have had or acquired had he or she not been so separated, subject to such time period and other conditions as the President may prescribe.

(3) An officer or employee entitled to reemployment or reinstatement rights under paragraph (2) of this subsection shall, while continuously employed by the Institute with no break in continuity of service, continue to participate in any benefit program in which such officer or employee was participating prior to employment by the Institute, including programs for compensation for job-related death, injury, or illness; programs for health and life insurance; programs for annual, sick, and other statutory leave; and programs for retirement under any system established by the laws of the United States; except that employment with the Institute shall be the basis for participation in such programs only to the extent that employee deductions and employer contributions, as required, in payment for such participation for the period of employment with the Institute, are currently deposited in the program's or system's fund or depository. Death or retirement of any such officer or employee during approved service with the Institute and prior to reemployment or reinstatement shall be considered a death

in or retirement from Government service for purposes of any employee or survivor benefits acquired by reason of service with an agency of the United States Government.

(4) Any officer or employee of an agency of the United States Government who entered into service with the Institute on approved leave of absence without pay prior to the enactment of this Act shall receive the benefits of this section for the period of such service.

(b) Any agency of the United States Government employing alien personnel on Taiwan may transfer such personnel, with accrued allowances, benefits, and rights, to the Institute without a break in service for purposes of retirement and other benefits, including continued participation in any system established by the laws of the United States for the retirement of employees in which the alien was participating prior to the transfer to the Institute, except that employment with the Institute shall be creditable for retirement purposes only to the extent that employee deductions and employer contributions, as required, in payment for such participation for the period of employment with the Institute, are currently deposited in the system's fund or depository.

(c) Employees of the Institute shall not be employees of the United States and, in representing the Institute, shall be exempt from section 207 of title 18, United States Code.

(d)(1) For purposes of sections 911 and 913 of the Internal Revenue Code of 1954, amounts paid by the Institute to its employees shall not be treated as earned income. Amounts received by employees of the Institute shall not be included in gross income, and shall be exempt from taxation, to the extent that they are equivalent to amounts received by civilian officers and employees of the Government of the United States as allowances and benefits which are exempt from taxation under section 912 of such Code.

(2) Except to the extent required by subsection (a)(3) of this section, service performed in the employ of the Institute shall not constitute employment for purposes of chapter 21 of such Code and title II of the Social Security Act.

REPORTING REQUIREMENT

SEC. 12. (a) The Secretary of State shall transmit to the Congress the text of any agreement to which the Institute is a party. However, any such agreement the immediate public disclosure of which would, in the opinion of the President, be prejudicial to the national security of the United States shall not be so transmitted to the Congress but shall be transmitted to the Committee on Foreign Relations of the Senate and the Committee on Foreign Affairs of the House of Representatives under an appropriate injunction of secrecy to be removed only upon due notice from the President.

(b) For purposes of subsection (1), the term "agreement" includes—

(1) any agreement entered into between the Institute and the governing authorities on Taiwan or the instrumentality established by Taiwan; and

(2) any agreement entered into between the Institute and an agency of the United States Government.

(c) Agreements and transactions made or to be made by or through the Institute shall be subject to the same congressional notification, review, and approval requirements and procedures as if such agreements and transactions were made by or through the agency of the United States Government on behalf of which the Institute is acting.

(d) During the two-year period beginning on the effective date of this Act, the Secretary of State shall transmit to the Speaker of the House of Representatives and the Committee on Foreign Relations of the Senate, every six months, a report describing and reviewing economic relations between the United States and Taiwan, noting any interference with normal commercial relations.

RULES AND REGULATIONS

SEC. 13. The President is authorized to prescribe such rules and regulations as he may deem appropriate to carry out the purposes of this Act. During the three-year period beginning on the effective date of this Act, such rules and regulations shall be transmitted promptly to the Speaker of the House of Representatives and to the Committee on Foreign Relations of the Senate. Such action shall not, however, relieve the Institute of the responsibilities placed upon it by this Act.

CONGRESSIONAL OVERSIGHT

SEC. 14. (a) The Committee on Foreign Affairs of the House of Representatives, the Committee on Foreign Relations of the Senate, and other appropriate committees of the Congress shall monitor—

(1) the implementation of the provisions of this Act;

(2) the operation and procedures of the Institute;

(3) the legal and technical aspects of the continuing relationship between the United States and Taiwan; and

(4) the implementation of the policies of the United States concerning security and cooperation in east Asia.

(b) Such committees shall report, as appropriate, to their respective Houses on the results of their monitoring.

DEFINITIONS

SEC. 15. For purposes of this Act—

(1) the term "laws of the United States" includes any statute, rule, regulation, ordinance, order, or judicial rule of decision of the United States or any political subdivision thereof; and

(2) the term "Taiwan" includes, as the context may require, the islands of Taiwan and the Pescadores, the people on those islands, corporations and other entities and associations created or organized under the laws applied on those

islands, and the governing authorities on Taiwan recognized by the United States as the Republic of China prior to January 1, 1979, and any successor governing authorities (including political subdivisions, agencies, and instrumentalities thereof).

AUTHORIZATION OF APPROPRIATIONS

Sec. 16. In addition to funds otherwise available to carry out the provisions of this Act, there are authorized to be appropriated to the Secretary of State for the fiscal year 1980 such funds as may be necessary to carry out such provisions. Such funds are authorized to remain available until expended.

SEVERABILITY OF PROVISIONS

Sec. 17. If any provisions of this Act or the application thereof to any person or circumstance is held invalid, the remainder of the Act and the application of such provision to any other person or circumstance shall not be affected thereby.

EFFECTIVE DATE

Sec. 18. This Act shall be effective as of January 1, 1979.

Index of Names

Acheson, Dean, 48, 60
Aesop, 45, 55
Aleutian Islands, 62
American Revolution, 28 *n.*
Angola, 6
Australia, 4, 8, 9, 10, 16, 44, 65, 66

Bauer, P. T., 5 *n.*
Bering Strait, 2
Berlin, 3, 47
Bolsheviks, 20, 23
Bonaparte, Napoleon, 61
Brandt Report, 51
Brazil, 6, 7
Brezhnev, Leonid, 20
Brown, Harold, 24
Brzezinski, Zbigniew, 38
Burma, 22

California, 7
Cambodia, 8, 16-18, 22, 26, 32
Cam Ranh Bay, Vietnam, 18, 26, 64
Canning, George, 32, 34, 35
Carter, Jimmy, 24-26, 30, 32, 34, 42, 43, 50, 53-55, 63
Castro, Fidel, 27
Chang, Maria Hsia, 57
Chiang Ching, 13
Chiang Kai-shek, 48
China, People's Republic of, 2, 3, 8, 13-28, 33-36, 40, 43, 47-50, 53-58, 60, 63, 65
Chou En-lai, 13
Church, Frank, 56
Cold War, 35, 47
Comintern, 15
Cultural Revolution, 8, 19, 20

Day, Peter, 51
Dulles, John Foster, 40

Egypt, 44
Eisenhower, Dwight D., 46, 47
England, 9
European Economic Community (Common Market), 12, 36

Ford, Gerald R., 54
Ford Motor Company, 23
France, 28
Fraser, Don, 53
Freedom House, 18, 22 *n.*

Gang of Four, 20
Gass, Oscar, 14, 34
Gastil, Raymond, 22 *n.*
Germany, East (German Democratic Republic), 47, 48
Germany, West (Federal Republic of Germany), 3, 45, 47, 48
Glendower, Owen, 35
Greece, 6,7
Gregor, A. James, 57
Gromyko, Andrei, 31
Guam, 32

Hawaii, 44
Hiroshima, 38
Hong Kong, 6-9, 11, 51

India, 22, 52
Indochina, 3, 10, 23, 30
Indonesia, 8, 16, 22, 30, 52, 65
Iran, 42

Japan, 1, 2, 7-11, 16, 20, 34, 36-46, 52, 55, 56, 58, 62, 64-66
Johnson, Lyndon B., 30, 31

Kahn, Herman, 15
Kennedy, John F., 30
Khmer Rouge, 18, 26, 27
Kim Il-sung, 27, 49, 60, 62, 63
Kissinger, Henry, 32
Korea, North (Democratic People's Republic of Korea), 8, 15 *n.*, 16, 18, 21, 27, 29, 48-50, 53, 58-60
Korea, South (Republic of Korea), 4, 6-11, 15 *n.*, 16, 24, 27, 29, 30, 37, 42, 43, 48, 49, 50-55, 59, 60, 62, 65, 66
Korean War, 2, 9, 27, 31, 40, 48
Kuomintang, 20
Kuril Islands, 58

81

Laos, 8, 22, 32
Lenin, Nikolai, 20, 26
Liberia, 52
Lippman, Walter, 3

MacArthur, Douglas, 3, 39, 62
McGovern, George, 34
Malacca Strait, 18
Malaysia, 6, 8-11, 22, 30, 51, 63, 65, 66
Manchuria, 38
Mansfield, Mike, 14, 33, 34
Mao Tse-tung, 20, 23, 26, 35
Marshall, George C., 2
Marshall Plan, 2, 3
Marx, Karl, 25
Mexico, 6, 7
Michael, Franz, 40
Mongolia, 2, 23, 39
Monroe Doctrine, 32
Mozambique, 6
Myerson, Adam, 45

Nagasaki, 38
NATO, 3, 14, 22, 36, 58
New International Economic Order, 9
"Newly Industrializing Country" (NIC), 6, 7, 11, 12
New Zealand, 4, 6, 8, 10, 16, 44, 65
Nixon Doctrine, 32, 33
Nixon, Richard M., 13, 24 n., 30, 32-35, 43, 50, 54

OECD (Organization for Economic Cooperation and Development), 12
Okinawa, 37
Okita, Saburo, 46
Oksenberg, Michael, 55
OPEC (Organization of Petroleum Exporting Countries), 6
Oxnam, Robert B., 55

Pax Americana, 10
Pearl Harbor, 1, 2, 38
Persian Gulf, 6, 11, 18, 31, 41, 42, 51, 61, 63
Philippines, 6, 8, 9, 16, 22, 37, 52, 62, 63, 65, 66
Pol Pot, 17, 26
Portugal, 6, 7

Red Army, 13
Red Guards, 20
Richter, Johann, 61

Sakhalin Island, 58
Saudi Arabia, 51
Shakespeare, William, 35
Shanghai Communiqué, 36, 50
Shigemitsu, Mamoru, 40
Siberia, 23
Sigur, Gaston, 40
Singapore, 6-11, 16, 22, 30, 51, 52, 65
Snyder, Edward K., 57
South Africa, 52
Soviet Union, 1, 2, 13-17, 19, 21-25, 34-36, 40, 48, 49, 54, 60, 63-65
Spain, 6, 7
Sri Lanka, 6, 22
Sukarno, President, 26, 30

Taiwan (Republic of China), 6-11, 15 n., 16, 24, 25, 27, 28, 36, 37, 42, 43, 47-58, 60, 63, 65
Taiwan Relations Act, 57
Tanzania, 6
Terrill, Ross, 25
Thailand, 8, 16, 18, 22, 26
Time Magazine, 34
Tonkin Gulf Resolution, 30
Truman, Harry S, 2, 3, 29, 47
Tucker, Robert, 5 n.
Turkey, 44

Uganda, 6
United Nations, 9, 26 n.

Vietnam, 8-10, 15-18, 21, 23, 24, 26, 27, 30, 31-33, 48, 50, 55, 64
Vietnam War, 3, 10, 15, 16, 30, 31, 33, 35, 54, 62

Walker, Richard, 21
Ward, Barbara, 9
Washington, George, 28 n.
World War II, 1-3, 7, 28, 30, 37, 44, 47, 63

Yugoslavia, 6, 7

Ethics and Public Policy Reprints

1. **Nuclear Energy Politics: Moralism vs. Ethics,** *Margaret N. Maxey*
2. **The World Council of Churches and Radical Chic,** *Richard Neuhaus*
3. **Western Guilt and Third World Poverty,** *P. T. Bauer*
4. **The United States in Opposition: Anti-Americanism in the United Nations**
   Daniel Patrick Moynihan
5. **Patterns of Black Excellence,** *Thomas Sowell*
6. **Why Arms Control Has Failed,** *Edward N. Luttwak*
7. **Environmentalism and the Leisure Class,** *William Tucker*
8. **A Search for Sanity in Antitrust,** *Walter Guzzardi, Jr.*
9. **Ethics and the New Class,** *Peter L. Berger*
10. **Will Lawyering Strangle Capitalism?** *Laurence H. Silberman*
11. **Is Capital Punishment Just?** *Ernest van den Haag*
12. **The Case for Doing Business in South Africa,** *Herman Nickel*
13. **Regulation and the New Class,** *Paul H. Weaver*
14. **Trendier Than Thou: The Episcopal Church and the Secular World,** *Paul Seabury*
15. **The Press and American Politics**
    J. William Fulbright, Raymond Price, and Irving Kristol
16. **Is the New Morality Destroying America?** *Clare Boothe Luce*
17. **Politicizing Christianity: Focus on South Africa,** *Edward Norman*
18. **Alienation and U.S. Foreign Policy,** *Paul Craig Roberts*
19. **The Cost of America's Retreat,** *Ben J. Wattenberg*
20. **The Soul of Man Under Socialism,** *Vladimir Bukovsky*
21. **What It Means to Be Number Two**
    Fred Charles Iklé, With a Response by Radomir Bogdanov and Lev Semeiko
22. **Dictatorships and Double Standards: A Critique of U.S. Policy,** *Jeane Kirkpatrick*
23. **Taiwan: Pawn or Pivot?** *Parris H. Chang, Gerald McBeath, and Ralph N. Clough*
24. **Crusade Against the Corporation: Church Militants on the March,** *Herman Nickel*
25. **America the Enemy: Profile of a Revolutionary Think Tank,** *Rael Jean Isaac*
26. **Washington vs. the Public Schools,** *J. Myron Atkin*
    Examines the increasing penetration of elementary and secondary education by the federal government to achieve social goals or to advance the interests of politically powerful minorities.
27. **Washington vs. the Universities,** *Daniel Patrick Moynihan*
    The senator asserts that the federal government has the power "to shut down any university" in America by withholding funds if it fails to comply with regulations tied to grants from Washington
28. **Christian Schools, Racial Quotas, and the IRS,** *Peter Skerry*
    The author concludes that the recent Christian-school movement is a reaction to "creeping humanism" and moral relativism in the public schools, not to racial problems.
29. **Solzhenitsyn and American Democracy,** *George F. Will and Michael Novak*
    Two respected political commentators admire Solzhenitsyn's insistence that an enduring society must have deep spiritual roots but find he expects too much from democracy.

Reprints are $1 each. Postpaid if payment accompanies order.
Orders of $10 or more, 10 per cent discount.